# EXTRAORDINARY

the world sold
you a map

what you need
is a compass

## Michael Dauphinee

BroadStreet Publishing® Group, LLC
Savage, Minnesota, USA
BroadStreetPublishing.com

## EXTRAORDINARY

the world sold you a map
what you need is a compass

Copyright © 2018 Michael Dauphinee

978-1-4245-5688-5 (softcover)
978-1-4245-5690-8 (e-book)

Stock or custom editions of BroadStreet Publishing titles may be purchased in bulk for educational, business, ministry, fundraising, or sales promotional use. For information, please email info@ broadstreetpublishing.com.

Cover design by Chris Garborg at garborgdesign.com
Interior by Katherine Lloyd at theDESKonline.com

Printed in the United States of America

18 19 20 21 22 5 4 3 2 1

In *Extraordinary*, Michael exhibits a unique style of captivating readers with real-life stories, allowing them to see themselves through this lens. He creatively assists readers to understand, digest, and utilize their strengths and foster meaningful, trusting relationships. Michael truly cares about people and encourages us to reflect on our own paths to success.

*—Dwight Powery, national site director, Year Up*

Mike's understanding of strengths and his practical, insightful focus on personal development provide a fantastic roadmap to those looking to add courage and clarity to their arsenal. I highly recommended adding *Extraordinary* to your reading list.

*—Nate Spees, CEO of Grizzly Inc.*
*and host of CreativeMornings, San Diego*

Michael Dauphinee is making a massive impact through his uncanny ability to speak to the heart with an authentic voice. His words resonate with a refreshing approach and resounding relevance in a world that desperately needs to hear what he has to say.

*—Damon Goddard, founder and director*
*of AMPD Golf Performance*

Working with Michael has been a life-changing experience. He has alternately nudged, challenged, and supported me through both big transitions and everyday leadership challenges. I have found his positive approach, impressive business experience, and strategic savviness to be the perfect blend for understanding the challenges executives face and coaching them to thrive in any circumstance.

*—Angela Titus, CEO of Cause Way*

Mike and his team helped us at a time when 78 percent of our staff had changed, and we were not performing as a team. In an industry that focuses on weaknesses, Mike helped us focus on our strengths so we could support each other. We reprioritized and reorganized, and the team became engaged in making a difference. Today, the organization is thriving and has made record improvements to the bottom-line metrics.

—*Curt Towne, former plant manager of Jefferson North Assembly Plant, Fiat Chrysler Automobiles*

Michael Dauphinee is a gem. Exceptionally bright, articulate, winsome, and passionate.

—*Alan Hirsch, author of* The Forgotten Ways *books*

For my relatives by blood and my family by choice,
I borrowed your belief until I could find my own.
None of this is possible without you.
Thank you, and may your lives be extraordinary!

# Contents

## Part I: IDENTITY
### Where Are You?

## Part 2: PERMISSION
### Where Are You Going?

# Foreword

By Paul Allen

I had my "Steve Jobs moment" in the summer of 2016. The moment came while I was on stage, speaking for two hours about the global strengths movement inspired by Don Clifton, the father of strengths psychology. The audience included many of the world's top strengths coaches from twenty-four countries. These were people who care deeply about helping others discover and develop their innate talents, creating fulfilling strengths-based lives. My friend Mike Dauphinee was in the audience.

I met Mike in early 2013. Since then I've grown to love him like a brother. He has challenged me—more than anyone else I've ever met—to be courageous. Every time I'm with Mike, I'm empowered with more stories and equipped with more insights. There's no question I want to be like Mike.

The peak moment during that keynote speech came when I mentioned Mike's work in the inner city of Costa Rica. He was meeting and coaching "leaders" of a particularly rough neighborhood. One of them was a fifty-nine-year-old sex worker who had sold her body for many years to provide for her four children but now, as a grandmother, had left that life and wanted to help others leave it as well. Mike showed her a Surface Tablet and invited her to take the Clifton Strengths assessment. Then, through a translator, he helped her understand what her strengths were. He asked her how she felt.

"I've never used a computer before. I like computers." And then, with tears streaming down her face, she said, "And your questions make me feel more human."

This story is impossible to tell without emotion rising to the surface. In the keynote address I told the audience, "*Every* human being born on this planet deserves a coach like that ... someone who cares ... someone who sees the intrinsic value in them."

Mike has coached nearly six thousand individuals in the last fifteen years. He works with an incredible variety of human beings: bank executives, CEOs, professional coaches, Olympic athletes, educational and nonprofit leaders in Detroit and DC, ex-prostitutes, illiterate doormen in Afghanistan, and many others. Mike sees each person as a genuinely valuable human being. He asks, "What talents does this person possess? What potential do they have? How can I help unlock that potential?"

A few weeks ago, Mike marked himself safe on Facebook after a bomb blast in Kabul. I wondered, how does he have the guts to keep going into a war zone to teach and inspire students and Afghan leaders? This book explains where Mike's courage comes from. It also shows what his courage and generosity have brought him.

From Samir to Isaiah to Abdul to Virginia, Mike's life is extraordinary and rich because his generosity encompasses every person he meets.

This is partly Mike's story. But it's also an invitation to reimagine our own story. Each point on his compass invites us to move closer to our own extraordinary life.

Mike Dauphinee is a strengths coach for the world. He wants each of us to live free, to follow our own compass, to cherish and nurture our relationships, and to live an extraordinary life. As our coach and guide, he gives us permission to be extraordinary.

—Paul Allen
*Founder of Ancestry.com and CEO of Strengths, Inc.*

# 1

# EXTRAORDINARY

To be nobody but yourself in a world doing its best to make
you everybody else means to fight the hardest battle any
human can ever fight and never stop fighting.
—*E. E. Cummings*

"Mike, I'm tired of not being able to tell the neighbors what you do. Ricky thinks you work for the CIA. I know you travel. I know you talk to people. I just don't think I understand what you do." I smiled at the classic dad question. He needed fodder for his friends. And while he was proud of me, he needed to nail down the details. The funny thing was that I struggled to explain my career as much as he did. But I tried. I gave my father the high points as I walked him back through the timeline he knew but didn't understand.

After college, a simple clicking mistake on a job site application led me to a position working as a resident counselor in drug rehab for convicted juvenile felons. Eighteen months later, when my student loans kicked in, I took a job answering phones at a call center for Hewlett Packard. In six years at HP, I saw success and promotion on the back of keeping promises more than business prowess. My realization at thirty of living a life offtrack had led me to pack up, leave San Diego, and move to Minneapolis. I spent more than a year volunteering with a small team doing leadership development for nonprofits. At a critical moment when I'd spent my savings and my student loans still called, instead of going back to corporate America I responded to a request from a director of a nonprofit in Detroit who had heard me speak. "Do you do consulting?" was a question that changed my life. I had no idea what I was doing, but that person became my first client.

One client led to another, I'd incorporated a year later, and the relational roots of my business took me from training to coaching and consulting. And after years of dealing with organizations in a variety of situations around the world, I'd been invited to meet with leaders at the Bill & Melinda Gates Foundation, the NFL, the US Olympic Committee, Fiat Chrysler Automobiles, United Way Worldwide, Bank of America, Microsoft, US State Department, and so many others. This string of experiences gave me opportunities to work in fragile and conflict-affected environments around the globe. I was traveling to places like Afghanistan, Nigeria, El Salvador, and Honduras. Everywhere I went, the process was the same, since every place had people. Assess individuals, give them the vocabulary to describe themselves, and coach leaders to lead: This was my method everywhere I went.

Dad listened as he drove, squinting from time to time to improve his hearing. As I finished, he said nothing. Then with the slightest head nod, he said, "So you help managers learn to help their people figure out what they're good at so they're happier at work and don't hate their lives." He'd nailed it. I smiled. After a long pause, he said, "Imagine the kind of a dad I would have been if someone had done that for me." It's the moments you never see coming that change your life.

My dad had few choices. A young family. No diploma. A terrible economy. The highest hourly rate and the potential for overtime was the only measure of a job that mattered. Choosing a position based on talent and passion was never a consideration. Providing was the priority. He worked as many jobs and hours as possible. And each night he'd collapse into his beat-up La-Z-Boy and let the TV wash the day away.

Driving to the airport that day, my father marveled as he glimpsed his alternate reality: A story where he worked for someone who wanted his best interest, and his work energized him. He came home happier. He thrived, and he balanced family with the demands of life.

Incredulous, he shared a recent realization. He now had open holidays and unlimited time off, but no kids at home to share them. His naked regret surprised me. Staring at the road, just above a whisper, he said, "What if someone had done that for me?"

There were no words. I sat in silence imagining that version of my dad's life. It would have been extraordinary.

Extraordinary is a great word. From the implications to the phonetics, I love it. It feels good. The fantasy of my happy dad, our enjoyable lives, the carefree days of childhood, the word *extraordinary* captured it all and made me smile. But like a rushing roller coaster dissolving beneath you as it crests the loop, reality grabbed hold of my delight. It was a dream. The truth told me what I already knew: His life wasn't extraordinary—or so I thought.

Dad's life was hard. He and my mom had survived, but it wasn't the pure joy I'd glimpsed in that breath. Staring out the pickup truck window at the endless northern Maine forest rushing by, I wondered how our lives ended up so differently. My life has often been described by my father as … well … extraordinary.

More often despite me than because of me, I've been able to live an incredible adventure. It has been rich and unexpected. It has been blessed and sometimes difficult. I've lived a story of notice. It's not uncommon to have people tell me how exciting, encouraging, and extraordinary my journey has been. And it has. Driving to the airport that night all those years ago, the realization of all I'd experienced and all my hardworking dad had missed planted a seed. I resolved that the fruit of my life would be helping as many people as possible to live the extraordinary life my dad never lived.

Cue the dramatic music.

I've told that story at speeches and workshops for years. It's my "why." I want to coach leaders to help their teams live extraordinary lives and thereby cultivate the extraordinary in all those they impact. I've used my love of the Clifton Strengths Assessment to help people understand their talents so that they can have this "extraordinary" life. I've traveled the world and taken people with me hoping a perspective-altering experience would lead clients to an exceptional life. I've mixed and matched content and exercises for more than a decade trying to concoct the formula for the alchemy of extraordinary. But I have discovered something striking. I didn't know the definition of the word extraordinary. That's a problem for a guy who uses the word "extraordinary" as the aspiration of his life.

In today's vernacular, "extraordinary" has become punctuation. It marks a thrilling point. For years, I've used the word to connote the unusual and unexpected—but always with a positive spin. I'm not the only one, and it's easy to see how it can become aspirational. We want extraordinary accomplishments, extraordinary love stories, and extraordinary lives—but only if they're positive, and that's nowhere in the definition.

Extraordinary comes from the Latin *extra ordinem* meaning "outside of the normal course of events."

That's it. Normal, not normal, there's no value judgment in there. The word is neutral.

Are you having a great hair day? "She looks extraordinary!"

Woke up with the Everest of zits on your chin? "That's extraordinary!"

Made the impossible a reality for a client? "You're extraordinary!"

Your boss is blind to your contribution despite the evidence of your effort: "He's extraordinary."

Jordan Spieth struggles on hole twelve of the Masters: "It was extraordinary!"

He shoots from the backside of media trucks, blind, onto the fairway, to come back and win The Open Championship in Scotland: "It was extraordinary."

Much like the word "leadership," we keep bending the definition in affirming directions. And if I'm honest with myself, that's why I liked it. I wanted leaders to care about creating a positive reality for their people. My childhood wasn't thriving like my current existence, so I needed a positive word. Extraordinary. But when I realized that there was nothing positive in the core definition, it felt cheap to make it an anthem. It sounded like the phrases said by people I despised: motivational speakers. (Want me to lose my mind? Call me a motivational speaker.) I hate when the glittering heroes of social media influence offer up content with the volume of cotton candy and just as much density. Words should matter, and my use of *extraordinary* didn't until I realized it did. I wasn't attributing too much to the word; I was ascribing too little.

Extraordinary: outside of the normal course of events.

> To live an extraordinary life is to live outside
> the normal course of events.

To live an extraordinary life is to *live* outside the normal course of events. It's about living beyond the circumstances.

It's an experience that transcends a trail or route. If I was going to advocate that people spend their essence in search of a life extraordinary, I needed to challenge them to reach for more than just positive feelings. It was about living above the transactional reality. Extraordinary life includes moments of pain, joy, success, failure, and everything in between, but we can use them as memorials more than guideposts.

We can't live on autopilot. Events are to be navigated, leveraged, and even stood on, but they're never to be bound to. I was trying to create a capacity for excitement and adventure in people by calling them to the extraordinary, but I was underselling the reality. I want you to live extraordinary lives not because you'll feel happy, significant, or adventurous. To live an extraordinary life is to live freely. It's living unbound from the courses others promote. It's finding the resolve to reframe reality, creating art from the mud of failure, and seeing events as things to be shaped, not surrendered to. It turns out my father lived an extraordinary life.

*To live an extraordinary life is to live freely.*

My dad was born in the small logging town of Patten, Maine. My grandmother had my father, the oldest of her three sons, just fifty days after her sixteenth birthday. "Man of the house" by age six, my father learned the realities of hard work. He spent many of his young years on the local dairy and potato farms that occupied any non-forested land around town. The story of a rural single mother of three boys in the 1940s and '50s could have ended with abandonment and despair, but it didn't. They often moved from rental to rental, but they always stayed together.

Introverted, fatherless, and one and a half times the size of every other boy in grade school, my dad was often the target of bullies. The threats reached the point where the teachers would let him out of school to get a head start as he ran home. When he was fifteen, my grandmother feared for him enough that she pulled him from school and put him on a bus out of town. She didn't know what was out there, but it had to be better than the life he was living. He got to Maryland and The Job Corp. The only white guy on a thirty-man crew, he worked the grounds at Camp David. A twist of fate and a crash course in etiquette landed him at a White House dinner escorting Lyndon B. Johnson's daughter and provided him a focus on table manners that I eventually learned to loathe throughout my whole childhood.

Choosing Navy enlistment over the Army draft, Dad was stationed in San Diego when not off the coast of Vietnam. He met (and later married) my mother after my great-aunt promised him Sunday dinner if he'd take her out. After the Navy, he found himself with a wife, two little boys, no driver's license, no high school diploma, and the worst inflation in US history. Dad took a job in a bagel shop and rode a bicycle in the dark to work every night. Believing they'd have a better chance in a small town, my parents packed their lives into a U-Haul (after my dad secured a driver's license) and drove the 3,445 miles back to my dad's hometown.

The population of Patten, Maine, in September 1975 was less than my mother's high school graduating class. While better in the long term, those early years in Maine were anything but easy. He got a job at the local plywood mill; then the mill burned down. He managed to get a house—the sewer pipe froze and broke in the middle of winter. While waiting for the mill to be rebuilt, he created multiple side businesses: welding, construction, making picnic tables. Years later he got the "good job" at the paper mill, but he then had to commute forty-five minutes each way, which required a car. He had multiple car accidents over the years due to weather, fatigue, or a combination of both. Looking back, I marvel at what a person can endure.

Sitting on a plane the other day, I thought of my dad at thirty-four years old. I don't know how he did it. He worked all the time. He would lie in the snow for hours welding on log trucks on some desolate backwoods road for a few hundred dollars. The winter of no toilet, my brothers and I would use a bucket that he'd have to haul deep into the woods late at night since there was no money to fix the septic line. He did whatever it took, physically and emotionally. I often wonder if I'm that strong.

Even as I write this, I marvel at how I missed the "extraordinary" in my dad's life all these years.

Somehow, we never had to move. My dad never left. He got his GED when I was in first grade and, before retiring, obtained certificates as a Class One welder who could calculate pressures and formulas in his head. His side jobs created a thriving and sought-after contractor business due to his quality and standards. He never cheated on my mother. He never drank. He never left. And the characters that ran him out of town as a boy now describe him as one of the most honorable men they know. I never realized it, but his life has been one lived "outside the normal course of events." Extraordinary.

It would have been normal for my young grandmother to abandon her child. My dad's torment should have made him an alcoholic. My parents should have split up. They should never have had children who earned college degrees, started their own businesses, and lived lives wanting to impact the world. But they did, no matter what the circumstance.

This hope is what I want for you. I want you to know you can live freely. You can live beyond your circumstances. You can treat the trials of your life as descriptors, not directives. But how? How was my dad not overwhelmed by events? Why wasn't I? It wasn't because his life was on track. No one offered him a path. He had no vehicle, and he had no map. In the end, all he had was an internal compass. While he didn't always know how we'd make it, he was still sure we would. While he may not have been able to articulate the destination, he was sure of his direction.

This is what I now offer clients who are navigating their most significant problems. I don't bring maps to success, and I can't build vehicles that will bring turbo growth to their business. We discover and refine a compass for their lives together. And while they may not always know where they are, they never feel lost.

Looking back on that ride with my father, my dad was right, but he was also wrong. He would have had a different life if he'd had a role and a boss that was there for him. But as I think of what he did and the compass he managed to give to me, his life couldn't have been more extraordinary.

# 2

# NAVIGATION

Complete freedom is not what a trail offers.
Quite the opposite; a trail is a tactful reduction of options.

—*Robert Moor*

I want to help you navigate in the direction of you. From our first breath to our last, each day is navigation, whether we realize it or not. Ordinary lives navigate by the normal events they experience. I want you to navigate past them. How do we do that?

The dictionary describes navigation as *the process of accurately ascertaining where we are, where we want to be, and making choices about how to get there.* It sounds like life. We're navigating. We don't talk about it in these terms, but it's what we're trying to do and the thing we muck up. Each section of this book is laid out by this definition: Where are we (*identity*), where are we going (*permission*), how we get there (*courage*), and how we keep from getting lost (*generosity*).

## Where Are We?

Our first problem is that step one of navigation is about ascertaining where we are. And it's not enough to have a sense of where we are; we need that sense to be accurate. People spend so much time seeking answers and resources to help them figure out where they're going but ignore the fact that they don't know where they are. I spoke at a conference in Ericeira, Portugal, a few years ago at a hotel on a point jutting into the ocean. The town is the westernmost point on continental Europe. A small fishing village, Ericeira had a legendary reputation as the home of the roughest and toughest fishermen in Portugal. I never understood why. As I walked around the beautiful alleys and squares, all I saw were wrinkled, smiling fishermen and homemakers greeting me. There were no wild men to be found. But the reputation of the town from time immemorial has been one of hard work and hard living. Stumbling into a map room at the resort one afternoon, I understood why.

On the walls were ancient seafaring maps and charts from the last 300 years. One of the oldest showed Portugal in all its glory, and there in the middle was the tip of the country sticking out into the ocean: Ericeira. But where the Atlantic should have been stretching outward toward Brazil and Central America, there was an open expanse covered in dragons instead. Ericeira was the home of the toughest of people because only the strong, brave, or crazy would be willing to live so close to the edge of the world where leviathan waited to devour you. They were sure they were in the shadow of mortal danger when instead they were colonizing one of the world's greatest surf spots. The first key to navigation is understanding where we are. Without this, nothing we plan will be accurate or possible.

Too many of us are living on assumptions of self based on the opinion of others, class expectations, and histories of failures. While these stories may have been true in the past, they are not a good basis for understanding today. It's not enough for us to say we know where we are before we start. How accurate is our understanding? Do you understand your identity?

# Where Do We Want to Go?

While knowing where we are can be a challenge, we seem to excel in looking for somewhere else to be. Since our toddler days when our sight went from blurry to clear, we've been reaching for things. Whether lights, toy giraffes, our fathers' beards, or anything our siblings had that we didn't, our vision and sight have been the drive for motion. This becomes more confirmed with age; it is as valid for emotional journeys as it is for physical ones.

We see things and move toward them. Sometimes the movement is for clarity, and sometimes it's for possession. Our vision determines our direction. But focusing on an idea as the sole priority for navigating life ignores something vital. Your vision is dependent on where you are. Your navigation plan will never be executed if it doesn't start from where you are.

Stand too close to something, and you miss the greater context; stand too far from it, and you fail to see the flaws. And there's a perspective-altering impact that results from different heights and elevations. If we start with a clear understanding of where we are, we can then take that into account when we start looking at the world. Others help us interpret what we see, but they can't see for us. We have to cultivate our own vision instead of buying it from others. Are you giving yourself permission to dream?

## How Do We Get There and Not Get Lost?

You may be one of the lucky ones. You may see yourself. You may have taken time to consider all the different views from your perch. You even picked a vision all your own. But how will you get there, and how do you keep from getting lost?

We get excited about our direction and satisfied with the rush of a destination, but it's rare if it ever becomes more than a dream. Navigating isn't about seeing a place you want to go. It's about going there before you die. I love Paulo Coelho's book *The Alchemist*. It's a fable of life on a journey. Santiago, a shepherd, sets out from Spain to North Africa in search of a promised treasure. He encounters challenges and struggles the whole way. Early in the story, he's sold his flock, left Spain, and made it to Tangier. A new friend steals all his money, and he's left penniless and alone. He talks his way into a job at a dirty crystal shop. The owner, having lost all motivation, agrees to let him work. Santiago cleans the items in the shop, sells them, and brings success to the shop and himself. The now happy shop owner, a kind Muslim man, spends his afternoons with Santiago drinking tea and talking about what they will each do when they have made enough money. Santiago dreams of home, and the shop owner dreams of making a pilgrimage to Mecca. It's the focus of their conversation every day.

One day, something shakes Santiago, and he decides he's become complacent, and he needs to go after his treasure. He gathers his earnings and goes down to the shopkeeper and says it's time. He says that he's earned more than enough money for his journey and his friend has more than enough money to take off for his pilgrimage. But despite Santiago's insistence, the man refuses to go. He tells our hero that they are different. "You want to realize your dreams. I just want to dream them." He's dreamed of his journey every night. What if he achieves it and it disappoints him? He would have nothing to live for.

The world wants to sell us a vision but has no interest in helping us realize it. They would rather you soak in it and, when you've had enough, go out and get a new one. Vision is important but useless without action. Doing what we've done will always get us what we've got. Navigation demands we move.

*We begin losing our momentum
as soon as we stop.*

I heard a speaker in college once say that drifting, dulling, and hardening had one thing in common: All that was necessary for them to occur was nothing. As soon as you kill a boat's motor, it drifts. When you stop using a knife, it dulls. And the moment you stop working clay, hardening begins. We have to keep the motion going. We begin losing our momentum as soon as we stop. But working for ourselves isn't enough. Our identity can start us on the way, but generosity will keep us going. This is how we navigate an extraordinary life in the direction of you. But if we're going in new directions, we need new navigation tools.

## The Problem with Maps

I love maps. They've covered my walls over the years. I like old ones, new ones, and the iPhone photo maps that show where my pictures are taken. Maps are affirming. We feel good about ourselves if we map out our plans. Maps are encouraging. There's an emotional rush at measuring our accomplishment. But maps are also comforting. If you've traveled and gotten lost, you know the wave of calm when a local says, "Don't worry—I'll draw you a map." It's too bad we can't use them. Maps are built on assumptions.

For maps to guide us, some things must be true.

- The mapper has to have been to our destination
- The mapper must know not only one route to our destination but all routes
- None of the conditions on the map can have changed since the mapper last mapped

Back to our definition of extraordinary life—living outside the ordinary course of events. While words like "normal" and "course" are hallmarks of a good map, they are also attributes of a mediocre life. You can't follow someone else's route to move in the direction of you.

But maps aren't our only problem.

## GPS Is Great for Groceries

In 2015, I had a brand-new, loaded Jeep Wrangler and three weeks with no clients. My first vehicle with GPS, I plugged in Alberta, Canada and drove out of San Diego. On a muddy logging road north of Banff and Jasper, Alberta, I learned that there are places you can go where even the satellites won't find you. Accepting assumptions and ignoring limitations are dangerous ways to navigate.

GPS is a great tool, but only for specific trips. Our GPS-navigated worlds only work with assumptions like these:

- The foundational map is accurate
- The system knows the fastest route
- "Someone" (satellite) is watching and always sees me
- Technology is more trustworthy than we are

In the Apple maps fiasco of 2012, Apple installed iMaps instead of Google Maps as their default direction software. The map data, being less robust than Google, was insufficient and incorrect. People followed their iPhones into lakes. GPS is good, but it has its limits.

The same is true for the tools of our lives. Apps for productivity, advice from friends, Instagram inspiration, and social media solutions are the personal GPSes of our times. They provide snapshots and possibilities, but you can't navigate the direction of your life by them. I get frustrated with the social media one-size-fits-all sponsored posts telling us to "Turbo charge your growth" or promising "Twenty-one days to bliss and contentment." The same tool that will help you find Starbucks isn't going to walk you through the politics of a hostile office. All the podcasts and Insta-stories won't silence your fear of being a fraud. And there is no productivity-tracking app for the courage to have the vulnerable conversation an extraordinary relationship demands.

We've traveled beyond the maps. The satellites can't see where we're going. But this isn't a bad thing; it's a new thing. We are living in an original time, facing unfamiliar trials. Some may call it frightening, but I call it extraordinary.

What do we do now?

To navigate the extraordinary and find the courage to live in the direction of you, you need new tools of navigation. Actually, you need an old one.

## A Compass

In 2010, I read an article by Guy Deutscher on the impact of language on thought. In it, he referenced anthropological studies of the Guugu Yimithirr aboriginal people of Australia. One of the unique attributes of this tribe was that their language had no egocentric vocabulary, only a geocentric one. Egocentric speech is critical to western communication—in modern navigation in particular. Egocentric navigation is direction-planning based on a person's present location. For example, we direct people to the restaurant by telling them something like "Go right at the light, straight for three blocks, turn left." It's assumed I'm not talking about someone else's right. You don't wonder if I mean the stranger in the crosswalk's left. Ego or self is the constant in modern directional language. The Guugu Yimithirr lacked this vocabulary, and therefore, tribe members held a perpetual understanding of "cardinal points" of direction (north, south, east, and west) to express everything.

Imagine living and communicating like the Guugu Yimithirr. What would it take? You'd have to think about directions twenty-four hours day. Left and right could be dangerous in travel and life. Imagine walking with your friend and having to shout, "Watch out! There's a python to the west of you!" Life would be lonely since most of your friends would be dead. The Guugu Yimithirr have a *compass* that never shuts off. The fascinating part of the article was when the researchers took geocentric language speakers, blindfolded them, took them to another city, into buildings with no windows, spun them around and told them to point north. They did, every time.

Deutscher remarked that non-egocentric speakers seem to have an "almost superhuman" sense of direction. Their understanding was ingrained from birth and didn't require practice or external factors for verification. It was an internal constant; *they just knew where they were.*

I told my friend Handel about the study. His face lit up. Handel is from the Tamil Nadu region of southern India. He said the "cardinal direction" language I was describing could be found in some villages near where he grew up. They use north and south instead of left and right, for example. But this type of communication is dying off. As younger generations have become exposed to the outside world, they don't retain their sense of direction. They've become more egocentric and need more egocentric directions. This is what's happened to us.

> *We don't need a map.*
> *We need a compass.*

We're dependent on ourselves. We think of directions regarding us. Our shortsightedness means we don't recognize that the steps and turns offered by the world can't get us where we need to go. We are charting a course in our direction and not to someone else's destination. We don't need a map. We need a compass.

## The Points on Our Compass

In an unstable world, a compass offers stability. The variability of your journey demands dependable touchstones. If the events that would tie us down can change, you need to understand values that don't.

The compass for the direction of you has four points:

- Identity
- Permission
- Courage
- Generosity

Not opposites like north and south, these bedrock anchors give you a constant sense of direction even to unknown destinations.

But a compass is no good unless you ping it. Ping is a submarine term used in navigation. It's what you do to verify something. We need to understand these cardinal points in our lives, but we also need to ping them as we walk. The following pages lay out the points for understanding each value and the questions to use to verify each one.

Part 1

# IDENTITY: Where Are You?

# 3

# DEFINING IDENTITY: THE QUESTIONS

Never forget what you are, for surely the world will not.
Make it your strength. Then it can never be your weakness.
Armor yourself in it, and it will never be used to hurt you.

—*George R. R. Martin*

The backed-up traffic sat waiting for the lights to cycle. Fiddling with the radio, I caught a glimpse of my face in the mirror. Bloated. Splotchy. My eyes looked like burnt holes in a blanket from too many nights of too little sleep. I froze. I was staring at myself but couldn't see me. What started as anger morphed into disgust, and by the time my watering eyes let go, I was gripped with fear. I couldn't escape the questions running through my mind. Who was that? That couldn't be me. That guy was unhappy. That guy was unhealthy. That wasn't my face. But if it wasn't my face, whose face was it? How could I not know the answer? How did I get here? Where was here? Alone in the car that pivotal morning, it was clear I had lost my identity, and I had no idea where to find it.

I told people I was doing great almost as often as I told myself. I'm not sure whom I was trying to convince more. My life had to be great. Business trips to exotic locations, a new car, respect at work, and life in the perpetual San Diego sun. The signs of success were everywhere you looked. It was the other signs I'd learned to ignore. Insomnia had become my shadow, TV was my closest friend, and my weight was on a steady march toward 320 pounds. I crafted a life with the description of success but none of the reality. Degree, job, zip code, and friends—on paper, it all looked great, as long as you didn't look at me. My words offered one story, but my face told another. I wasn't looking for a change, but the need for one was staring back at me.

Our plans will never get executed if they don't start with where we are. When I finally reached my starting point, I wasn't sure of where I was going, but for the first time in a long time, I could see where I was. What I feared was the end was actually the beginning.

## Identity as True North

Everything has a starting point, and ours will be identity. Our plans will never be executed if they don't start from where we are. Identity will be our true north, the most significant point of our compass. The first step in navigation is to ascertain where we are with accuracy. We have to start with this question: "Who am I?"

This question is as simple as it is complex. Our identity is the embodiment of the axiom "the whole is greater than the sum of its parts." I could list personal features of my identity as on a driver's license:

Height: 5'11"
Weight: 250 lbs.
Hair: Brown
Eyes: Blue

While each fact is a component that describes me, if it's separated from all the others, it's not me. My height is a fact about me, but I can't use it to navigate my life. My eyes are blue, but that doesn't make me better suited for a role. This is a simple idea, yet we often miss the correlation with trying to do the same thing in other areas of our life. Job, degree, age, fame—each can be elements that are a description of you, but they are not you.

But this is too complicated for the speed of our world. I used to have a colleague who said that a confused mind says "no." Rejection is our default to anything too complex to understand. We like simple, and so we seek simple definitions for ourselves.

We define ourselves today with our personal brand: social media followers, degrees, vacations, jobs. But there are two problems. First, those things are not cardinal or unchanging parts of you. They are trend-based and unstable. The sign of prestige today is out of favor tomorrow. Your identity and the starting point for our plan has to be the dependable core of you. This is the accuracy part of our navigation definition. To start our plan, we need a stable starting point. And second, any aspect you offer the world is meant to *describe* you, not *define* you.

Imagine you're looking out an old frosted window with four panes. You can see through only one pane. You tell everyone there is a beautiful green yard out there, and you should all go fly a kite. As another pane clears, you change your mind and realize there's a giant tree in the other half of the yard, so kite flying is a bad idea. Let's all go for a walk. As the remaining window clears, the rest of the nearby forest is clear … as are the mother black bear and her two cubs. Maybe you should all just stay inside. There is a yard, but there's also a tree, a forest, and wildlife that shouldn't be messed with. We can't offer the world fractional understandings of ourselves and then complain we're misunderstood. Identity encompasses you, and it's the dependable you. But how do we define it?

# Defining the Terms

There's an old proverb that says, "The beginning of wisdom is to call things by their right name." I want to give you words to describe your identity so you'll know what you're seeking. I'll flesh them out in the coming pages, but here's how they come together.

Your identity is like a triangle. There are three sides: Talent, Purpose, and Passion. These pieces are reliable, they snap together, and each is incomplete without the other.

*Talent* involves our naturally recurring patterns of thought, feeling, and behavior. Do you pick someone to race when driving? Do you start conversations with strangers? Do you have trouble sitting in restaurants with your back to the door? Do you hang your shirts in the closet according to color and sleeve length? Do you see houses on hills when driving and imagine the lives of people living there? These thoughts, feelings, and behaviors are natural talents. No one told you that you have to do that. You don't wait for others to approve. You feel what you feel and think what you think. And barring pain or constraint, you do what comes most naturally. This describes your talent.

*Purpose* is the application of your talents. It is the thing to which your thoughts, feelings, and behaviors can be applied. People often argue with me about this. The modern vernacular is that purpose is a motivation or driving inclination. When it comes to the core of our identity, the thing you're searching for is the classic definition of purpose: The reason for which something was created or done or for which something exists. Purpose can be a motivating factor, but I'm pushing for the application definition.

*Passion* is the final side of the identity triangle. Passion is a strong and barely controllable emotion. Passion is what gives identity its magnetic pull. It's a unique sight to behold, but when passion joins talent and purpose, this alignment of identity creates incredible momentum.

To better understand, imagine a knife.

## What is the purpose of a knife?

What constant elements must a knife possess to be a knife? A handle, a blade, and an edge. If any item lacks any one of the three features, the tool is no longer a knife. A handle, blade, and edge: These are the talents.

What is the purpose of a knife? Its job is to cut. We could use it as a screwdriver. We can use it as a wedge to lock a door. It can even be used for scraping and cleaning. But the real purpose for which a knife exists is to cut.

But what a knife cuts best is dependent on passion. It's something so obvious and apparent that it almost defies any other application. Can you cut a two-inch ribeye steak with a scalpel? Yes, but a scalpel would be better used for saving a human life. There are many overlapping applications of purpose, but it's our passion that makes us unique.

The gravity that will draw you toward extraordinary is the mass of talent / purpose / passion pulling together and anchored to your soul. But if it's so intense and vital, how do we lose it? Can you lose your true north?

## Which Way Is North?

For a compass to work, the index point, the directional arrow, must be magnetized. The electrons in specific materials align naturally and are drawn to particles moving in the same direction. The most reliable natural magnetic force on Earth is what's called magnetic north. The arrow of a compass is always moving toward this giant magnet. This force is strong enough that you can stand anywhere on the planet, and a magnetized needle will point north. North is the point by which all other directions are derived. North would be Earth's identity. So is it possible to lose your north? How can we lose our identity? The answer may surprise you: We can't.

Your identity is constant; it doesn't go anywhere. But when it comes to navigation, we can start following fake forces. If you put another magnet near a compass, the proximity of the outside force is strong, and the directional arrow will swing toward it. This is how we lose our way.

You're born with a clear sense of self. You exist. You have characteristics. You have abilities. You have appetites. But we aren't careful about what we expose ourselves to. We start to consume media. We hunger for the sugar rush of others' praise. We let the gravity of comparison drag us down roads we never imagined. We pick majors that others want for us. We take jobs that impress our peers. We buy things we can't afford. While we're doing all this, we wonder why we don't feel like ourselves. We're responding to the draw of the things we've allowed near us. We've got to ask better questions and resist false offers.

We need to do the archeology of our own lives. We need to hunt for our original understanding. We need to find ways to verify the purpose for which we were created. And then we need to go about the difficult work of removing the dust and clutter that has buried our identity and masked the gravity calling to us. An archeologist finds value in the original, the core, the forgotten. They look to foundational purposes and discern the real from the forgery and appreciate the authentic even when marked with scars of life. You've got to be an archeologist of self if you're going to find an identity to guide you in the direction of you.

## Identity: The Answer to Your Question

As the next few chapters clarify each element of our identity, like the action stars of our favorite adventure films, we're going to have to get dirty, shake off the dust, and reassemble some things long broken or unused. So break out your work clothes. But before you start digging, take time to start asking.

The process of owning your identity begins with questions. Who am I? How did I get here? What things in my life magnify the gravity of my identity, and what things are trying to mask it?

> *While I did not yet have answers,*
> *it was enough that I was asking the right questions.*

In the fourteen years since I pulled down the off-ramp to work and stopped running the race of someone else's life, I've discovered a truth. You have to start with the questions. And waiting for my turn at the light, seeing my angry, tear-stained face in the mirror, I learned something that has comforted me ever since. While I did not yet have answers, it was enough that I was asking the right questions.

# 4

# TALENT

Hide not your talents, they for use were made.
What's a sundial in the shade?

—*Benjamin Franklin*

When I was thirteen years old, I got the dream job of every thirteen-year-old boy in Patten, Maine. I became a bag boy at Ellis' IGA. I loved being a bag boy. I loved customers. I loved loading up paper bags and carrying them to the cars. And the two-minute walk to the parking lot was my show. "Is that a new perm, Mrs. Merrow?" "Like that Buick, Mrs. Landry!" Talking to customers was my thing. But mopping floors and dusting shelves were supposed to be my things too. It didn't matter, though, as long as I could talk to customers.

After a few months, I got called into the manager's office. I wish I could say I didn't remember his name, but I do. It was David Cunja. It was my very first "manager talk." He sat me down and said to my glazed face, "Mike, you seem to like talking to customers more than you like mopping floors." This guy understood me. Wow. I never realized he was so amazing and such a true man among men. "You're right, Mr. Cunha." I was lucky to have a good boss.

Smiling, I waited for his next words. He was perplexed. He tried again. "Mike, you talk a lot." Yes, sir, I do! This guy was my friend.

Realizing his mistake, he cut through the fog. "Mike, you could keep this job if you didn't talk so much."

I can still feel the pit in my stomach as I walked down the ramp to the parking lot after handing over my apron. It felt like freefalling. I didn't understand. I felt overwhelming shame. I didn't "get it" until I did. Over time, the lesson became clear.

Having a job was good, and not having a job was bad. People who didn't talk had jobs, so they were good. I talked and didn't have a job, so I was bad.

> *The key to becoming all I dreamed I could be*
> *was in figuring out what not to be.*

The mind of a thirteen-year-old is uncluttered, and tough lessons last. Here's what I learned that day. The key to becoming all I dreamed I could be was in figuring out what not to be.

I grew up being called "motor-mouth." I talked too fast. I said too much. One woman from church took it upon herself to proclaim in front of my family and friends that I chewed my words, and that she was going to teach me how to talk one summer.

Worse, I was quick to speak and slow to think, and that's an unfortunate combination for a child of conservative parents who loved the phrase, "Children should be seen and not heard." Comments from others were bad enough, but having a boss hand you a failure for doing something that came like breathing was devastating—but instructional.

But it wasn't just the IGA. Bullies are good at shaping behavior. I was mocked for how I talked. I was called unspeakable names. Even Mr. Martin (his real name—never pick on an author!) ridiculed me in front of my seventh grade English class. "Hey, class, I bet Mike can't go twenty minutes without speaking. If he does, you have homework; if he doesn't, you get the night off." The public scorn of your friends in seventh grade, facilitated by a teacher. Brilliant. It's a good thing junior high isn't hard at all.

Every day, the lesson was reinforced. I'll be liked, loved, and employed if I just stopped talking. I'll be all I want to be if I can just stop being me. It sounds foolish now, but I'm not alone in my folly. We are all trying not to be something.

## What Are You Trying Not to Be?

You can tell what you're trying to not be by the words you use to describe your behavior. I never said to myself, "I need to work on being less expressive." Instead, I said to myself, "Don't be a blabbermouth." We use negative, shaming language when we "coach" ourselves on what to not be to become what we dream of being.

You're not neat; you're obsessive. You're not responsive; you're flaky. You're not innovative; you're unrealistic. You're not introverted; you're insecure. You're not relational; you're emotional. Our words betray how we feel about ourselves.

Our drive to "become by not being" starts early and lasts long. The first twenty years of life provide the imperfection we need to remove so that we can live the lives of our dreams. While almost anything can drive this negative behavior, two areas get the most attention: difference and defense.

The threat or experience of isolation for something you think, feel, or do is a powerful motivator. I didn't know I had a speaking problem until my manager called it out. And once I saw it, it was all I could see. If that was in the way, if that was what was keeping me from success, I needed to focus on it to get rid of it. What separated you from others?

You felt like the fat kid. You had curly hair you wished was straight. You were the only one of your ethnicity in class. You played in the band. You were poor. You were rich. You talked too much. You got good grades. You got bad grades. You were too religious or not religious enough. Many people spend their lives trying not to be whatever they feel makes them different. But that's not your only option. Others build a defense against shame.

We try to prove opposites. We're the opposite of every bad thing we think we could be. It's impossible to make this case, but we don't care.

We can't be seen as a loser. We can't be seen as lazy. We can't be seen as imperfect. We can't be seen as uncaring. We become obsessive, demanding, and defensive as our default. If no one ever says it, we'll never be it. So we try to prove we're the opposite of irrelevant.

But whether running from what comes naturally or running from what we're afraid of being, it doesn't matter. We're still running away. But as the saying goes, "Wherever you go, there you are." That doesn't stop us from attempting self-surgery.

## The Scoop of Success

I learned in my twenties that I couldn't stop being something. I wasn't strong enough. I'd coach myself to not speak up in public, to be less opinionated, and to be more disciplined. Restraint was the key. It would work for a time. I'd talk less. I'd tick off fewer people. Then something would happen. I'd run my mouth. Someone would get mad, and someone would cry. Like a wild horse, my mouth would go the way I wanted until my arms got tired of holding the reins. I'd give up, feel shame, retreat, but try again. What else could I do? It was a hopeless cycle. Over time, I recognized that restraint wasn't enough: Success required removal. I didn't need to shape what was inside of me. I needed to scoop it out. This action became my focus.

I remember standing in my kitchen one evening washing dishes, replaying a night gone wrong in my head. I had said something careless, and a friend and his wife drove away in anger and tears. Standing at the sink, overwhelmed with shame, in brokenness I prayed, "God, if you're the creator of the universe and you can do anything, why can't you scoop out this jerk inside me and pour someone valuable in?" It never occurred to me that he already had.

Scooping is our preferred method of dealing with anything we want not to be. We learn in the early years of professional development that restraint is unrealistic and only removal will do. Carve it out. Deny all impulse. Don't trust yourself. Look to others before you look to yourself. Despise anything that sounds like your voice. Become a personal skeptic, and over time, you will excise the defective parts of yourself that are standing in the way of your success. And once you've scooped out your insides, you'll finally be ready to pour value in.

We pour in value in a variety of ways. We adopt other people's habits, reach for their approval, and seek suggested degrees so we can upgrade our thinking. We listen to the right influencers, belong to the right societies, and walk the steps of a successful world that has the answers we could never hope to possess. When Gallup asked respondents what the key to professional success was, over 70 percent said identifying weakness and fixing it. Scoop out the bad, pour in the good. But it's not true. You cannot scoop your way to success.

*Talent can't be scooped. It can only be shaped.*

Talent can't be scooped. It can only be shaped.

In the early 2000s, I was a volunteer leader at a community nonprofit, and we were going to use a new assessment to help mobilize our volunteers. Gallup, mostly known for polling, had recently stepped into performance management with an instrument that's now called Clifton Strengths. I'd never heard of it, but like everyone, I love to hear about myself. After sitting through the workshop on Gallup's research and assessment accuracy, I was ready for my packet.

I waited until I was alone to dive in. I skipped the top sheet and began reading. I read one, then another, faster and faster. I became so angry I stopped reading. These results couldn't be right. The assessment was called Clifton Strengths. It was supposed to be a catalog of what was right with me. But as I read my packet, I didn't see strengths I'd developed but flaws I worked fifteen years to discard. It had to be wrong. It had to be. Those stupid questions couldn't have led to these words. I talked less. I was more thoughtful than ever. And I was less opinionated and reactive than I'd ever been. I knew I was. My career was on the upswing. I was getting recognition, rewards, and all the accolades that came with them. All because I'd scooped out the useless habits in my life and, through hard work and education, had poured my value in.

Glaring at my Clifton Strengths Signature Theme Report, I despised what I read. It was clear that I was a failure. My flaws had gone nowhere since they were staring back at me on paper.

Communication—my best hope was in speaking and helping others to find their words.

Command—my desire for things to be led well will help others to achieve.

Activator—while often impatient my drive for momentum helped keep things from being stuck.

Woo—the spirit of friendship that turns any activity into a positive moment.

Positivity—the gift of believing that almost anything is possible if we just keep the faith.

That's what the report said. All I saw was this:

Talkative.

Opinionated.

Careless.

Attention seeker.

Sucker.

## What Is Talent?

One of my many client workshops is on strengths and team performance, and I open every session the same way. I have people stand up, find a partner, and then I give them three questions for discussion, one at a time. I may vary the first two, but the last one is always the same.

"Name one thing you do better than anyone else you know."

From Honduras to Nigeria, I've never had a crowd not groan. I wait for the nervous laughter. They shuffle. Most come up with something, but there's always a few that give up. It's a question of talent. What do you bring to the table that no one else can supply? This question stumps people for two reasons: Some don't see their talents as unique, and others, like me, resist valuing things they've tried to remediate. To rediscover our identity and calibrate our compass, we need to start declaring our talents instead of working to discard them.

> *We need to start declaring our talents instead of working to discard them.*

Talent, as defined by my friends at the Gallup, is *naturally occurring patterns of thought, feeling, or behavior that can be productively applied.* It's things we think, feel, and do that become useful. They're not choices but patterns. Talents are hardwired. Talents are instinctive. Talents are established in our brains during the most formative years. Talent is the raw element on which everything else is based. Talent is also ignored, misunderstood, and taken for granted.

Our desire not to isolate drives us to assimilate. Our assumptions are rampant. We think the truth is true, and that if it's true for me, it must be true for you. This belief lets us miss our talent because if I think, feel, or do something, so does everyone else. We believe there is nothing special about it and nothing unique here. We don't see our natural ability as anything worth focusing on.

We think everyone gets joy from cleaning their garage. We're sure ordinary people profile the cashiers at Costco to identify the fastest one. It's a given you're supposed to pick someone to race when driving. And of course, strangers tell you their life story after you greet them with "Hi, how are you."

Talent is the reliable core of you. It is the alchemy of your family, friends, and your environment from the first twenty years of life. It is the hunger stirring in you when you feel the need to speak, the drive to create, or the compulsion to bring order to a chaotic world.

Shape, don't scoop.

Looking at my Clifton Strengths report, it laid out all my talents. It put words to things I felt but didn't know how to name. And despite my feelings about them, they couldn't be denied. The science was sound, and the research was true. This list of talents described how I thought, felt, and often behaved. But instead of being something to be scooped out, they needed to be shaped. I wondered if it was true.

Could I contribute to the world not by removing or adding to myself but by refining what was already there? I began to think about it. Gaining knowledge, skills, and experience wasn't wrong; it was necessary. But instead of replacing my talent, knowledge, skills, and experience are meant to shape it. Education can never replace a lack of talent. Not everyone can be great at everything. Practice doesn't make perfect. Talents practiced can become perfect. But this isn't what we do.

A number of years ago, I was consulting for a large nonprofit in Boston. It was a yearlong program. During one of my coaching sessions, one of the executive vice-presidents proclaimed to me that he understood this "shaping, not scooping" concept. He led the communications department but had only recently begun to give public speeches in the city. Most of his days were filled with meetings and planning. His speeches, however, were a hit. Others were telling me about the impact they had, and how the community leaders were inviting the EVP to address different crowds because he was so good. And he loved giving the talks. Our discussion of talent now made sense to him.

He told me that during his performance evaluation with the CEO the next week, he was going to propose hiring a speech coach to become even better. This would elevate the organization in ways that hadn't been planned but to more significance than expected. He would use his development dollars to shape his talent.

He was miserable during our next visit. After meeting with the CEO and sharing his plan, the CEO laughed in his face and said, "The only thing I'm willing to pay for is organization and time-management classes because you don't respond to email on time." Good idea, send your valuable resource off to a class to learn how to be less annoying to you. Don't invest in something they're great at that could be beneficial. Shaping is about how you're applying resources to the core of you. It's either refinement or removal.

The problem is that if you remove or discard your talent, it has to be replaced by something. The identity triangle won't snap together with just anything. This is a foundational problem that effects all navigation that comes after. We have to ascertain where we are to plan navigation. We can't plan from where we want to be. We need to shape, not scoop. But what are we shaping?

I don't care what you use, but we all need words. You need to know what your talent is made of to select the right tools to shape them into strengths. Find an assessment. Some use the Myers-Briggs, DISC, or Enneagram. I've made Clifton Strengths the song I sing. The research is world-class. The emphasis is on leveraging what's right with people not what's wrong. And the focus on thoughts, feelings, and behaviors allows the tool to be used in more productive ways.

You need to realize you're talented. You need to stop discarding your most valuable parts. Continue to seek knowledge and personal development, but not to fix what was never broken. Talent is the platform that your identity is built on. You can't trust the magnetic draw of your personality if it is variable. You have to believe that there are reliable parts of you and that this is your talent. The beautiful, unchanging, raw humanity that calls out great possibility. Don't throw it away. Cherish it, refine it, and see what it can do. You'll be amazed. I was. Many mornings, as my plane takes off, I catch myself thinking that the thing Mr. Cuhna fired me for is the very thing clients pay me to fly around the world to do today.

# 5

# PURPOSE

The purpose of life is not to be happy. It is to be useful, to be honorable, to be compassionate, to have it make some difference that you have lived and lived well.

—*Ralph Waldo Emerson*

As I mentioned, my parents spent many years just making things work without a lot of money. From raising our own chickens to buying leftover potatoes from local farmers, we were organic, homegrown, and homemade before any of it was cool. And I'm certain the conservation ideals to repair clothes and not buy new started with my mom and had nothing to do with the environment.

My mother is a woman of many talents, not the least of which is stretching pennies. When it came to clothes, she was the master. She made most of her own. We shopped at Sylvia's resale shop in Brewer, Maine for many childhood back-to-school shopping days, all before vintage was cool. You got used to the sneakers bought two sizes too big and the jeans that had to be hemmed so they could be unhemmed as you grew. For better or worse, she could fix it all. Definitely for the worst was pajamas.

We always had footie pajamas. Blue, yellow—and one year,

one of us three boys got pink. They were on sale, and they were all that was left. "No one sees you in your pajamas, so who cares?" was my mother's response. We'd have them until they wore out. But wearing out was a rare event. Nothing was ever so worn that mom's sewing machine couldn't fix it. She was great at fixing things. A broken zipper? Fix it. Hole in the armpit? Fix it. Torn cuff? Fix it. Most of the time, you didn't argue and just put up with the old pajamas and went to bed. Who cares? But everyone has their limit.

I don't remember how old I was, but I was old enough to know that footie pajamas were not a good thing. With the risks of the pajama zipper in all of its terror and the perpetual annoyance of sweaty feet, I was not a fan. And entering a growth spurt, my latest pair was starting to become more and more uncomfortable. The seams cut into my shoulders, and my toes crammed into the bottom. "No problem," she told me one morning; she'd fix it. And she did.

That night I took them out of my drawer, put them on, and began howling. "Mom!"

My complaining got louder and louder until it interrupted Dad's TV, and he demanded to know what the noise was. His annoyance melted into laughter as I marched into the living room in yellow fleece PJs with no feet. She had cut them off. That would have been bad enough, but by removing the pressure point that was holding this masterpiece together, the lack of fit was revealed as the leg holes now strained almost to my knees. And the back seam was so far up my poor behind that I almost needed pliers to remove it. When my dad stopped laughing, he agreed that the issue was no longer about fix but fit. There it is.

Purpose is the question I get asked the most about. People are hunting for jobs that will lead to success. They've taken Clifton

Strengths and want me to tell them how to fix their careers. They were great in college and aced the job interviews, but two years in, they are miserable and merely middle-of-the-pack performers. They don't know where they went wrong, but they're sure they did, and they want me to help them fix it. Unfortunately, not everything can be fixed.

## It's Not about Fix but Fit

Because we ignore our talents, we build professional lives on our knowledge and experience. We sell the world our degrees. We see each role as a step to another. Our contribution to the world is built on the refined application of all the good we've poured into ourselves over the years. It seems like a good plan. It's everyone else's plan, so it must be the right plan. Gather something to make yourself significant, find someone who wants what you gathered, and sell it to them for a price that will make you happy and fulfilled.

You have a degree in communications. You took a job in a drug rehab center right out of school to help make a difference. HP needs a customer service representative who can handle demanding customers. The salary will cover student loans and rent. You take the gig. See the formula? Does it sound familiar? It should work; it should be good, and it is—until one day, it isn't.

Something happens after nine months. You're taking 200 calls a day, your supervisors are happy, the bills are paid, but there's something wrong—it doesn't feel like enough. So you begin looking for other roles.

You discover an inside sales support role. Since you have a PR degree in communication and now you have company experience, and since the new manager needs someone with your understanding of needy customers, they're willing to help you cover even more of your bills.

Of course, in twelve months you'll feel the nagging which means that you've got to fix your professional plan and make another change. You remix the formula again. A new division, your degree, a call center job, an inside sales support job—it can now be spun into a customer contracts administrator, then a contracts manager, and eventually a global contracts negotiator. Others call you tough and ambitious, but you're an obsessive fixer. Until one day you're pulling down the off-ramp on the way to work, and you catch a glimpse of your face in the rear-view mirror …

The problem is most of us think we have careers that need to be fixed when we're living lives that don't fit.

> *You need to figure out the thing inside you*
> *that you value most.*

Purpose is about an application, but it's the application of our talents, not all the tools that we've gathered to shape our talents. We offer the world our collection of high-end hammers and chisels, ignoring the fact that they need a sculpture. Not everything can be fixed, especially if it's not broken. Your career isn't something in need of repair. You need to figure out the thing inside you that you value most. Find a place that wants the product of that talent and only offer it to those that will appreciate it. But we don't appreciate things that are broken.

We live in a culture that believes personal and professional development are an endless cycle of fixing. Of course, we believe we're broken. In school, we had "progress reports," which should have been named "lack of progress reports" since the focus was always on what wasn't working. At work, "areas for growth" had less to do with being more productive and more to do with being less disappointing. And when Gallup surveyed parents around the world with a question about grades—"Your child comes home with a report card of one A, two Bs, a C, and an F. Which grade deserves the most attention?"—you know what grade parents around the world answered in an overwhelming majority.

*Do not confuse a lack of failure for success.*

I had a friend complain I was ignoring a valuable tool in fixing. I told her it's about what you're trying to achieve. If you want to not fail at work and life, focus on fixing your annoying habits. But do not confuse a lack of failure for success. Success only comes from the perfect application of talent, and that's all fit.

The problem is once we start fixing, we can't stop. We've invested too much to turn back. This is what my psychology colleagues call *equity saving*. We can't let go of people and situations because we think we can save our investment in them by investing even more.

You buy a car you think is going to be just what you need, and it's a decent deal. But one day, an oxygen sensor goes dead. You replace it, and a few months later, the timing belt is squealing. You spend a few thousand to get it fixed. Before long, the AC dies. You have it recharged, but it doesn't solve the problem. They replace the coil only to realize the compressor fan has a glitch, and they want to check to see if the thermostat needs replacing. In a matter of months, you've spent more on car repairs then you paid for the car. But instead of cutting your losses, letting go of the car and finding something more reliable, what do we do? We say, "I can't get rid of it—I've invested too much." We continue to invest more resources to justify the resources we spent. It's a vicious cycle, but we can't help ourselves. It reflects the heart of our belief that everything can be fixed if we just push hard enough.

I've had many clients who refuse to fire disengaged employees because it would be a waste of training and management investment. It already is. They're not performing, and every day you keep them near other, you increase the chance that the disengagement and frustration will spread. Keeping staff who are actively disengaged convinces your engaged employees that you don't care about performance. But we've worked so hard to fix them; we don't want to admit our mistake and let them go. If you can't fire them, pay them to stay home. But here's the problem: Most disengaged people are not looking to be fixed; they're just in the wrong fit.

We are at our best when see a clear application and purpose for our uniqueness. Our purpose feels like a perfect fit. The only way to find what fits is by trying things on.

## What Size Are You?

Discovering the purpose of our talents is like finding a fit for the core of you. The word *fit* describes the way two things are in alignment or harmony or even the way they match. And when it comes to fitting your purpose for your talents, there are a few things we have to keep in mind.

We need to get honest. I'm a guy, and studies show guys usually think they look better than they do while women think they look worse. Maybe you have an uncle who proudly proclaims he still has a thirty-six-inch waist like in high school—but his jeans are headed south because the overhanging gut is forty-four inches. You'll never find things that fit if you can't be honest about who you are.

I was with a new client the other day. The CEO of a manufacturing company. He's a young guy who just took it over from his father. He was excited to tell me all about a new product they were going to rush to market to capitalize on a competitor's mistake. It was totally new, they'd never created anything like it, and it wasn't in the plan we discussed one month before. When I asked how the machine shop was going to feel about the increased workload, he assured me they're great. They love working for us. We have a pretty happy team. I asked again, knowing they'd struggled with hiring a needed fifteen additional employees for manufacturing for better than a year. He insisted it was all good. But when I kept asking how he knew for sure, he just kept quoting his intuition. We need to have the truth reflected back to us from more than one source. How do you know what fits? Who is giving you feedback that this is you at your best? Honesty is developed in community. I'll talk about this in the *permission* section (Part 2), but until then, avoid assumptions—both positive and negative.

Many people take assessments like Clifton Strengths and love their results. They're encouraged and empowered, and they can't stop talking about them. But there are a lot like me who hated their report. They didn't like what it reflected because it reminded them of something they didn't want to see. Too often, I meet people who cling to fitting purpose to their degrees and experience because they dislike their talents so much they don't believe anyone would find them valuable. Some people struggle to understand their flaw while others won't embrace their genius.

"My themes are so boring."

"It sounds like I'm a cartoon character."

"Basically, it sounds like I'm a jerk."

We have to find ways to make peace with the truth. You have naturally occurring patterns of thought, feeling, and behavior that are unique to you. These talents are tools. They are morally neutral. There are no good talents, there are no bad talents, there is only what you do with them. Stop resisting using them in your life because you misused them in the past. Your dad may have yelled at you for playing with matches as a little kid, but that doesn't mean you refuse to light a fire when camping. We need to stop pretending our talents aren't valuable, embrace them, and find new ways of using them in our lives.

Some people struggle to find a fit for their talents because they deny they're of any value to the world. Others struggle because they're convinced they're God's gift to the world. These people have been doing what they do their whole life naturally and are confident in the truth of their perspective. This can be true for many reasons. Because of our talents, we are sometimes blind to some things and laser-focused on others. For people I meet who are totally ignorant of those around them, lacking all relational talent, it's a lot like being colorblind to the needs and emotions of others. When you realize a person can't see colors, you make allowances for that person, but it doesn't mean you let them pick out your socks.

There's a loss in those who can't see their talents, so they don't understand who they are. But an even more painful experience is being around people who are so entitled they can't see who they are *not*. Connecting talent to a purpose that fits is about seeing and valuing what your talent is, but it's also about what it is not.

## You Stink at Things!

You stink at things. It's okay. We all do. We typically don't tell you because we're nice. You've got to find a way to be okay with what you're not. You are not perfect. You don't have all the answers. Too many young entrepreneurs are exhausted with worry about what they are not and try to make sure the world doesn't see them as a fraud. Vulnerability is tossed out the window for bullet-pointed press releases about how great they are. It's a lie. And in the mirror in the dressing room, I can stand there and suck my gut in for a minute, but that doesn't change how I look walking on the street when others see my clothes are too small.

Fit is about alignment and harmony of different things. If you build jobs, companies, and relationships around the fake version of you, everyone will feel the pain when you stop sucking in your gut.

Fitting your purpose cannot happen until we are willing to see ourselves clearly. We need to stand in front of the mirror without shame, without self-deception, and embrace what we are and what we are not—and then go find some clothes in our size.

If the first step to finding our fit is embracing our true talent, then the second is trying things on. You've got to be willing to test out options.

## Try It On

A significant number of one-on-one meetings I do are with people in their late twenties and early thirties. They have all the potential and all the hang-ups you'd imagine. But one thing I've found is that with each passing year, they feel more and more pressure to make sure every professional decision is the perfect one. I tell them that they'll never know if it fits until they try it on. I bought a new, expensive carry-on bag right before my latest international trip. Unfortunately, I bought it online without ever seeing it in person. I was sure it was fine. It was supposed to be the same dimensions as my old bag. Well, it was—but only after opening the expanders. The night before a twenty-day trip to Dubai, I was cramming everything in, angry at the cost of this thing that didn't fit. This is why online stores are getting more generous with returns. They know people like to test things out before they commit. When it comes to your experiences, you've got to give yourself permission to try things.

We're talking about using identity as the true north of our compass. You have to ping or test out your directions to see which way is north. Have you seen hikers holding a compass as they turn right and left, watching the arrow move? They're testing to see where they are in relationship to their target and determining their next steps. Will they get nearer or farther from their direction? You have to do the same. Apply for jobs you may not want. Attend conferences that may not be in your specific field. Don't avoid all tangents. See them as testing things out.

Treat negative experiences as things you get to cross off your list. Every crappy boss adds to your list of things to screen for in your next interview. Every deal that goes bad is one more example of people you don't want to partner with.

We can't find a purpose that fits if we can't see ourselves with clarity. We'll never find a good use for our talent if we don't try things out. But the last factor in fitting is understanding that what fits today may not fit tomorrow.

## What Do You Want to Be When You Grow Up?

When you find the right application for your talents and you begin to apply them, something incredible happens: You grow. You get better and better at what you do. Practice doesn't make perfect; practicing your talents makes perfect. Once we've found the roles and opportunities that seem to be tailor-made for us, we think we are done looking, and we can relax. The good news is that we will start to grow. The bad news is we will outgrow the places we planted ourselves.

> *The good news is we will start to grow.*
> *The bad news is we will outgrow the places*
> *we planted ourselves.*

The application for our talent is something that is dynamic and will need to be refined the rest of our lives. Our talents aren't changing, but our use of them is.

When I incorporated my company in 2006, I didn't have a business plan and couldn't describe what I did. All I knew is that I had left HP, spent a year working for pennies for a university in Minnesota to learn Clifton Strengths, and now people were willing to pay me to come do Strengths workshops. I would do sessions with anyone and everyone. I taught Strengths in churches, schools, living rooms, and even on a college leadership program that was a race through Europe. I was all Strengths, all the time. I was using my talents of Communication and Positivity.

But in a few years, workshops started to be less satisfying, so I began to offer to help clients onboard their new employees. I still did workshops, but I needed something more. Workshops became consulting, and that became coaching. I still do all these things, but now I'm focused on the fact that my products have to help clients solve their most significant problems. I don't coach just anyone. I won't work with leaders who aren't interested in solving problems. I have told multiple clients if they're looking for team building as motivation, send the crew to a resort. To hire me would be a waste. I'm way too expensive, and I don't do spa days. Today, I think I'm one of the most proficient Clifton Strengths consultants in the world, but my purpose isn't Clifton Strengths; it's helping people solve their most significant problems.

I'm not limiting our discussion to purpose. Can you hear it in my description? Talent is what we do naturally. Purpose is the application and refinement of our abilities. But for these elements to become our identity and a gravity we can walk toward, we need to own our passion. We need to know what moves us, what makes us strong, and what painful things we never need to do again … like wearing outgrown footie pajamas.

6

# PASSION

Human beings are not primarily thinking creatures.
We are creatures driven by our loves.
—*Matt Chandler*

"So I was crawling down some back alleys with six little kids,
trying to dodge the machine gun fire … yeah, that's when I
decided I liked helping kids." Ah … yeah.

I had done this exercise many times but never in Afghanistan.
It was my standard passion exercise. I told my group of twenty
students we were going to do a timeline exercise. I wanted them to
draw a line on a notebook sheet. On the left side they could make
the end as far back in their personal history as they wanted. The
right side was the present day. Then I said they should mark on
the line the three or four events or people who had had the most
significant impact on their lives. They could be positive or negative, but they had to be impactful. When done, they were to create
three or four bullets telling why each milestone made the line.
Then they had to craft a paragraph about how these bullet points
shaped the type of contribution they want to offer the world. They
got into it.

I sipped my thousandth cup of tea for the day waiting for

them to finish so we could do a report-out and I could make my point about "Identity-Based Leadership." It's pretty easy to get into a routine and forget where you are when teaching the same topics over and over. Even in Afghanistan, despite it being a war zone, I had found a routine traveling back and forth since 2010. Over the years, I've heard a variety of responses in the timeline debriefing, but they fall into patterns. Divorce, sports, a mentor, moving, public affirmation. Machine gun fire was a first.

As Imram relayed his story like he was describing a Tuesday, I worked to not react with astonishment, to honor the fact that, in a place like Kabul, he was describing Tuesday. He had been working at a community daycare center on the compound of the new Afghan Parliament. There were about thirty-six kids and four or five staff. Listening, I remembered the news coverage of the event a couple of years before. There was a Taliban attack on the parliament that lasted hours. Gunmen climbed into a taller building under construction nearby and launched a rain of grenades and gunfire at the parliament building. As the parliamentarians fled the compound in their armored SUVs, Imram and his coworkers were left trying to evacuate all the children from their building, which was between the gunmen and their target.

Breaking them into groups of five or six, each staff member took a collection of kids and, for the next few hours, crawled and ran through bushes and alleys to deliver each child to their home. As if he was describing his favorite color, he said, "So that's when I decided I liked helping kids." These are the moments when passion is born. Talent is unique. It's a combination of patterns like eye color, height, or hair. Purpose has overlap. You can use different talents to be an incredible project manager or an incredible teacher. But passion is a fingerprint. Yes, everyone has them, but no two passions are the same.

# Why Are You So Emotional?

Passion is a strong or even barely controllable emotion. We dismiss emotions as nothing more than untrustworthy feelings. Emotions are irrational, personal, and hard to label and catalog by our data-obsessed world. Jobs and schools hate emotions. It's easier to teach to the masses if we condition kids to put their feelings aside and want what the teachers want. Companies assume you'll receive as much satisfaction filing reports as they do getting them. And if you aren't happy, if you're frustrated or discouraged, it's because you're emotional or not the right person for the job.

I once interviewed a vice president of development at an influential nonprofit in Silicon Valley who'd had 90 percent of her team quit the previous year. When asked the reason for the turnover, she said, "They're all so emotional. People today want to have their hands held." Her words were harsh but not uncommon. Most organizations prefer their people to not have feelings or emotional opinions. They need to come to work, do what they're told, and not expect the boss or their colleagues to be their friends.

We've arrived at this cultural place with integrity. During the industrial revolution, the start of organized work as we know it, there needed to be a better way to move people into jobs and training. It required mass influence and leadership scaled to a level that society had never known. The historic parent of today's organizational structures is the military. It goes further back than the Romans.

How do you get masses of people mobilized and moving in one direction to accomplish a target or goal? You have a single person in charge of many and replicate the model in cascading fashion. And with each drop of the leadership waterfall, you limit the scope of responsibility and mental contribution of individuals.

By the time you get to the bottom of the chain of command, all the poor guy knows is how to hold the pointy stick in front of him and go in one direction when he's told. Did that guy know who he was sticking with that spear? Did he feel like marching that day? Was he sure the guy he was killing was the right guy? Questions like those would get you stuck with a spear yourself. And let's not even consider emotions. You couldn't have those! Individual feelings were disruptive to unit cohesion.

Try to tell organizations from churches to governments and start-ups to corporations that they're militaristic, and they'll let you know that you're crazy and uninformed. But it's a rare thing to find an organizational culture that isn't hostile to individual passion and emotion. Rarer still are ones that seek to be emotionally engaged environments. Most are leading people like they're marshaling infantry. Make it simple, make it pointy, move in a specific direction. Logical and efficient are the demands of our lives.

## Passion Is Disrupting

We have learned to repress or ignore our feelings and emotions because they don't fit well into the organized plans of others. Too many leaders want to gather followers that will conform. I was talking to a Strengths coach some years ago. I told him I was going to offer one of his contractors some extra work I didn't have time for. "I know it would help out his finances, and I'm sure you're fine with him refining his passion." The guy angrily said, "Absolutely not! To be on my team, he needs to be excited about my passion." Ah ... yeah. I'm all for people being aligned with vision and mission, but you'll never replace anyone else's passion with your own.

*You can never run on someone else's passion because the source of passion is your own feelings.*

The "feelings" component of Gallup's definition of talent is too overlooked. Talents are patterns of thought, feeling, or behavior that can be productively applied. *Feelings.* You can never run on someone else's passion because the source of passion is your own feelings. And these unique feelings are something to be developed, refined, and offered to the world. If you embrace this, it will disrupt your life.

You'll work harder. You'll give more. You'll demand less. You'll do things for reasons other than money. You'll become frustrated with people who are "paycheck players." You may be less logical. You may risk more.

I started traveling to Afghanistan in 2010. I was invited by a friend of a friend. There was a team of doctors and teachers that came in on a regular basis and provided medical and leadership training for various audiences. The Command side of my Clifton Strengths talents was thrilled to be invited. Anyone can help in tranquil settings, but I relish the hard. The trip changed me.

I fell in love with Afghans. I loved trying to contribute in any way possible to a world trying to improve itself in desperate conditions. I met students at a leadership organization called Afghans for Progressive Thinking—APT for short. They drank up every conversation like wanderers in a desert. I also got to do leadership development sessions with the international aid groups working across the country. The people I met stole my heart, and I began trying to find ways to get back in the country as often as I could.

The next few years' trips were sporadic and pro bono, but by the end of 2014, I had an actual contract with American University of Afghanistan, Kabul to consult for a business incubator for Afghan entrepreneurs. December 2014 was a tense and stressful time. That month, the contentious and protracted presidential election had been resolved. The majority of US coalition forces were officially ending combat operations and leaving the week before Christmas. And I had begun receiving emails from the US State Department warning of the increased threat of kidnapping of internationals from my neighborhood in Kabul. Then, five days before I arrived, the situation got worse.

An international non-governmental organization, one focused on educational development, was attacked, and both the director and his two teenage children were killed. The humanitarian NGO community in Kabul is small, and the tragedy created shock waves. Aid agencies pulled their staff out of the country, and those that remained were on lockdown. I received the news thirty-six hours before my scheduled departure. I wrestled with the decision. It was unnerving on the one hand but felt all the more necessary on the other. The NGO teams that were restricted to their houses would need more support despite fewer being available.

My process in making big decisions is to think, spin the ideas, then talk it out with my friends. That had always worked before, but this time it was different. I was concerned, but I was leaning toward still going. As I talked to people, I underestimated their level of concern.

The attack made the news, and my friends were concerned. But still *feeling* strongly about it, I began telling people I was still going to go. I'll never forget a call with one of my oldest friends. In tones I'd never heard from her before, she said, "That's a terrible idea. Nothing you do there will be worth your life!" And she wasn't alone.

I couldn't believe my friends were saying this. After years of talking about service and sacrifice, I tried to treat everything like it was worth my life. Otherwise, what was I doing? They had always agreed and encouraged me, but now their words were empty talk. It took an emotional toll on me, and I questioned a significant decision I felt clear about for one of the few times in my life.

Looking back, I recognize that most of those comments were

said in love and with a desire for my well-being. But I've learned something when it comes to navigating choices for my life: My tolerance for risk has a direct connection to my level of passion. And this tolerance, while based on my feelings and emotions, makes others uncomfortable. I make no apologies. As my passion for people in fragile and conflict-affected environments has grown, my decision-making has been disrupted. I've never made my day rate on any international job. Eighty percent of all my international work has been free, and I pay the expenses. But as my need for revenue has increased, I find myself agreeing to do more global work, not less. I don't say that for affirmation, but as a declaration. Passion has disrupted how I make decisions in my life.

If you start listening to your feelings and embrace them as a tool in decision-making, it will disturb your life, and not everyone will understand. It's okay; they don't have to. You do. You have to know the source of what impacts you—the nuances and the expression of the things that motivate you. In the extraordinary life, this is a nonnegotiable. You have to recognize, endorse, and grow the things with the most substantial emotional connection because if passion is going to be a binding force in your identity, it has to be something strong enough to sacrifice for.

## The Price of Passion

I grew up in church. I love the story of Jesus. But when I was a little kid, it never made sense to me that the Easter Sunday church skit was called a "Passion play." Was Jesus supposed to be excited about dying on a cross? He never looked happy about it in the pictures. The word never seemed to fit. Someone eventually explained that a secondary definition of the word passion was the suffering of Jesus. The word passion that we throw around so much in society is from the Latin meaning "to suffer." It gives new context to the masses saying, "I want to be passionate." Really? You want to feel suffering? Okay.

The meaning has changed over the years, but there's value in retaining the concept of suffering in the definition to help us separate passion from emotions. We have feelings about things every day; most depend on our mood, circumstances, and interactions with others. Feelings are healthy, they're real, and if we listen, they can be valuable tools in managing our growth. But how is this different from passion? The answer isn't in suffering. It's in sacrifice.

Passion is a value or belief that is persistent, significant, and ingrained deep enough that it is worthy of sacrifice. I have profound feelings about ice cream, but I'm not always willing to get up and walk to the store when the craving hits me. Feelings don't equal sacrifice. Our passions are deep emotions but in a way that makes the sacrifice of other things reasonable. What are you willing to sacrifice for?

I worked with a guy in Detroit who ate one meal a day so his kids could have three.

I knew a man in Costa Rica who sank his anemic personal savings into starting businesses that only employed prostitutes and convicts.

I know a trekking guide in Chilean Patagonia named Roberto who worked the trails for fourteen years to put his siblings through college and one through law school.

I know a nurse at the Veteran's Hospital in San Diego who chooses to work in certain wards for the financial stability it allows her family, so her husband can work with the refugee community.

What's worth taking night classes for? What do you give up your free time for? What indulgence will you pass on? What career opportunity is worth a cut in pay? Will you rent instead of buying to have more flexibility? Is there a calling so deep that it means you choose to adopt instead of having biological children?

Will you pass on a new iPhone to build your savings to have more options? Will you live in a different neighborhood so your kids have friends with different ethnicities? You don't understand your passions if you don't know what they cost.

> *You don't understand your passions*
> *if you don't know what they cost.*

Too many people are sacrificing, but they're doing it for someone else's passion. A parent, a mentor, a spouse—if you don't have a passion, it's easy to grab theirs. But it's not sustainable. Passion is based on an emotional feedback loop of the energy. While our passions demand everything, we end up getting back more than we give. But if you sacrifice for the passion of others, the more you sacrifice, the more it gives to them. This is fine as a start, but your well will run dry. So how do we find your passion?

## Let's Go to the Replay

To keep the emotional engagement of passion free from the tangled feelings of today, we've got to look back to yesterday. Passion isn't built in a single moment. It's not one feeling. Passion is like the redwood trees of California. As each individual sapling grows, its roots begin reaching out to other trees and creating a network stretching more than one hundred feet from the trunk. With an interlaced foundation, a grove of trees can be strong enough to withstand the fiercest storms. It's the same with passion.

Moments mark the timeline of our lives. Set deeply enough, they take root and reach from one meaningful experience to the next. These impact points connect and intertwine, creating a passion that is an amalgamation of the people, experiences, and events that mark our lives. The first step in grasping our passion is to look back at the moments that made us.

In their brilliant new book *The Power of Moments: Why Certain Experiences Have Extraordinary Impact*, brothers Dan and Chip Heath talk about how single instances shape the course of our lives. Often the most powerful moments are found in "pits, peaks, or transitions." We are marked by the high points of success and experience, the low points of desperation, and the transition points between. This is the framework I provide clients when we do their timeline exercise. If they're struggling with what makes the timeline, "pits, peaks, and transitions" is an excellent primer.

Once you've looked back at the "replay" of your life for the moments, now you need to see what that story is telling you. Cut out all the other years of your history. If these moments were playing in clips like the dramatic montage when the world has been saved at the end of the movie *Armageddon*, what do you feel? What emotions come up? What does it drive you toward?

Are you angry, so you never want anyone to feel what you felt?

Were those moments you felt most understood?

Did you feel connected and safe?

Do those times remind you of being challenged and the satisfaction of being your very best?

The moments on the timeline merge to produce powerful feelings that make up one half of our passion. The other half of our passion is people.

Who do you want to protect, advocate for, create experiences for? Passion always has a people element. It was moving to watch interviews with the actors and producers of the Marvel movie *Black Panther*. In one press panel, Chadwick Bosman, the star of the film, was moved to tears retelling messages from young fans. The whole crew wanted to create a great story, modern art, something escapist for a world in need of distraction. But great work wasn't enough. The passion that moved this man to tears was the recognition of what it means for little kids who are not white to see heroes that look like them. Being an actor that tells exceptional stories may be his emotional driver for life, but his passion is the impact his art has on a young audience.

Feelings that drive us can feel like passion, but until they connect with others, they're nothing more than emotions. Passion's partnership with emotion and people comes in the maturity of understanding our story and the gift it can be to others.

The north of our compass is complete. You have innate talent and ability. Refined and matured, your talent needs to be applied to meet needs that fit. And then the impact that fits will be multiplied when it's directed by your passion. Put the three together, and you've got a compass. That compass may not help you dodge bullets down the dusty alleys of Darlulaman Road in Kabul, but it is a compass that will lead you to you.

# 7

# NORTH STAR / COMPASS

Why is it that we don't worry about a compass
until we're lost in a wilderness of our own making?
—*Craig D. Lounsborough*

They called her Didi. She was nobody. She didn't want to be any-
body. She spoke to few. She lived a solitary existence. And after
the death of her sister in the early '80s, she had no family to speak
of. She lived her life, and that was enough. So her passing alone
in September of 2010 surprised no one. It was the expected end
of an unremarkable story. What was remarkable was what they
found in her cottage in the British countryside. Looking through
her papers, they discovered Didi was Eileen Nearne. The name
was not significant, but the Croix de Guerre medal awarded by
the French government after World War II was. After a government search, it was discovered that Eileen was one of thirty-nine
women who were picked by Churchill and dropped into the
French countryside in World War II as British spies.

Fluent in French, she operated a vital radio relay between the
United Kingdom and the French resistance. The first time she
was captured by the Nazis, she talked her way free by convincing
them she was a foolish simpleton being used by an overpowering

French man. Caught a second time, she was sent to a concentration camp. After escaping, she was recaptured, tortured, and sent to yet another camp—and then escaped again, hiding out until the American troops arrived. And then the Americans held her as a spy too until confirmation of her identity reached them from London.

The *New York Times* reported that British debriefing documents said "the Gestapo tortured her—beating her, stripping her naked, and submerging her repeatedly in a bath of ice-cold water until she blacked out from lack of oxygen. They failed to force her to yield the secrets they sought: her real identity, the names of others working with her in the resistance, and the assignments given to her by London. At the time, she was twenty-three."[*]

During an interview in London when asked how she didn't break, she said, "The will to live. Willpower. That's the most important. You should not let yourself go. It seemed that the end would never come, but I always believed in destiny, and I had a hope." Those who understand their identity are never without hope.

> *Those who understand their identity are never without hope.*

Do it for you.

When you navigate your life by your identity, you have a point to guide you and a reason to hope. You have a north star all your own. And as you cross terrain that no one has ever walked, you will be able to make choices that no one has ever made. Make the decisions that reflect who you are, not who you hope others will see. You will endure what others see as intolerable when you have a true north to guide you.

---

[*] John F. Burns, "Eileene Nearne, Wartime Spy, Dies at 89," *New York Times*, September 21, 2010, https://www.nytimes.com/2010/09/22/world/europe/22nearne.html.

Too many of us confuse "get to" with "have to." They're chasing perfect performance, but not because it's stimulating, exciting, and powerful for everyone around them. People are chasing perfection because they won't know who they are if others don't think they're perfect. My friends with the Clifton Strengths theme of Achiever struggle with waking up every morning feeling like they *have* to "earn their shower." But what if instead of compulsion, it's a reward? What if they treated it as an energizing gift they get to use instead? Don't confuse what you do with being you.

> *Don't confuse what you do with being you.*

Life is meant to be an expression of your talents and passion, not the evidence. When you shift from living your life to justifying your life, the truth is that you've stopped living.

We have a habit of putting our identities into the hands of others. It's like we take out our heart, hand it over, and then beg people to tell us it's beautiful and valuable. We have to put our identity back into our chest. You are not your metals, your awards, or the opinions of others. You're not your task list. You're not the perfect business plan. You're not your first round of funding. You're not your ability to conceive a child. You're not even your ability to raise a considerate one.

We spend so much time crafting the credentials of a valuable human being that we forget to focus on being one. I used to have a client in downtown Detroit who loved to have meetings about meetings. One team, in particular, was led by a guy who liked to call meetings about the planning meetings to discuss how he was going to message the progress to the public. He used the word *optics* before anyone else I knew. Talking about work was more fun than doing the work. If that was problematic for me as a bag-boy, you could imagine the impact as a vice president. I used to say to him over and over, "If you would just build the skyscraper, you'd never have to spend time telling people what you made." He spent $65,000 to throw a public party to celebrate achieving 65 percent of a five-year goal. He built the talking points of impact but was never impactful.

I always wanted to shout at him: Be trustworthy. Be resilient. Be creative. Be critical thinking. Be industrious. And in the end, if no one else knows, who cares? Navigating your life for the response of others is like trying to drive a car looking back over your shoulder. Before long, you will hit someone or drive off the road. But repeating these sentences as a mantra won't change anything. To start to live by your identity, you need a core belief: The belief in a question.

## Questions Only You Can Answer

According to Viktor Frankl in his landmark book, *Man's Search for Meaning*, there was a transformational power in living in constant questions. A psychiatrist imprisoned in the concentration camps of Auschwitz and Dachau, he became fascinated with understanding why some people survived unspeakable horror and others would die of despair. In his research, which became known as Logos or "meaning" therapy, he saw that people who questioned everything—themselves, their health, where they were being moved or what was going on in the war—anchored themselves to a future hope. But of all the things that kept people walking down this road that no one had ever walked, there was one question that stood out from the rest.

The toughest people in those hellish places were driven by a sense that they needed to go on living because life would ask questions that only they could answer. It was a possessing belief that if they didn't survive, things would be left undone. Stories would be untold, and the piece they were meant to contribute would leave the puzzle of life incomplete. This belief is living guided by your identity.

When Didi was laid to rest, she had lived quietly following her identity and hope and did it for no acclaim, but the obscurity she sought for years was lost. The newspapers broadcast her story around the world. Veterans from across the country came. Twenty-two standards were lowered by honor guards as her casket entered the chapel accompanied by the Consul General and a military attaché from the French Embassy in London. For sixty-six years, she never told her story. It would be up to the lives she changed to share it for her.

What if we all did the same?

What if we made passionate decisions, created a new purpose, and never apologized for being us?

We can let the pieces fall where they may. And like Didi, we'll leave it to the world to tell our story.

Part 2

# PERMISSION: Where Are You Going?

8

# DEFINING PERMISSION

Our chief want is someone who will inspire us
to be what we know we could be.

—*Ralph Waldo Emerson*

The year 2012 was an exhausting one for me. I created a new, comprehensive, talent management program for a client, had twelve-week stretches of travel at a time, and was burned out. One night that fall, I was speaking at a retreat center high in the Rockies north of Pike's Peak. I had made it through the day, but it hadn't provided the energy it usually gave. Lying in my bed that night, surfing the glacial Internet on my phone, I knew I needed a break and decided I was going to Machu Picchu.

I'd never been to Machu Picchu, but it's where people said they were going when they said they needed to get away. I began searching for trekking companies and trips. I found a company called Oneseed Expeditions. They're a Denver-based global expedition company that hires native guides, profit-shares the trips with them, and puts 10 percent of revenue back into the local community in microfinance loans. Founded by Chris Baker, a Yale grad who worked for Kiva in Nepal in the Khumbu region below Mount Everest, Oneseed was now branching into Chile.

Oneseed was running a discount for their inaugural South American expedition called Epic Patagonia. Who needs Machu Picchu? I had no idea where Patagonia was. But before falling asleep that night, I'd registered, paid, and was dreaming of Patagonia peaks. Five months later, racing past the Guanacos as the dust poured into the fourth bus of the day, the dream felt more like a nightmare.

I had signed up to join a hiking group. It was my first communal travel experience. I figured I could hide out in the back of the crowd and go slowly. As the months went by, I made an effort to get out and hike. I was putting miles on my boots on weekends. I've always been more of an endurance guy than a sprinter, and so I thought I'd be fine. But as the date got closer and I read up on what we were doing, I grew concerned. This was the Torres del Paine "W" route. It was about ninety kilometers, it was to be done with a full pack, and it was "hiking through" (after the first night there would be no roads out). After recovering from a stress fracture, I was running again and watching my diet, but I wasn't convinced I was ready or had logged enough miles. I grew up hiking and fishing but hadn't been in touch with my outdoor roots for some years. This could get ugly.

Six weeks before my February 1 hike date, the Oneseed office called. Due to a fluke of scheduling, all the other hikers in my group had rebooked to different dates. Did I want to change too? I had clients scheduled before and after, so I couldn't. The initial flash of disappointment gave way to relief when I realized they'd be canceling my trip for lack of numbers. It would be for the best. The last thing I needed was to get stranded on a mountain in Chile. But then she said, "No problem." Any other time, they'd cancel, but since it was the inaugural season, they wanted to keep the date. If I were okay with it, I'd have a personal guide for the entire expedition. I coughed and said, "Great." The deposit was nonrefundable.

My guide Roberto Carlos deserves a book all his own. After our plane fought the infamous Patagonia winds into Punta Arenas, Roberto Carlos Bahmenodez strolled up to meet me like an icon out of *National Geographic* magazine. He had a huge red pack, well worn and repaired with care. He wore worn, La Sportiva trail shoes, harem pants, and an over-fuzzy, black fleece jacket. Around his neck on a leather strap hung a stone fossil of a prehistoric sea creature he'd found while guiding a group of paleontologists. And on his head was his trademark round, black, and red knitted cap, like the ones worn by old horsemen on the ranches or estancias up and down the Patagonia range. I could tell he was sizing me up, but his smile and laugh put me at ease.

His English was much better than my Spanish, but that doesn't mean much. He managed to brief me while we waited for the three-hour bus ride to Puerto Natales. Digging out his ever-present map, he traced our route and pulled pictures of things we'd see along the trail out of a Ziploc bag. Birds, trees, and his prized picture of a puma. I understood about 60 percent of what he was saying. The two of us would be alone on the trail for seven days; this was going to be fun.

The rush of arriving melted into genuine concern as we got ever closer to the national park. After checking in and picking a bunk in the Las Torres Refugio, I went outside to stare up at the world-famous granite spires of Las Torres peeking over the ridge surrounding our camp. That would be our destination tomorrow. I can count on one hand the number of times I've felt that level of distress. How was I going to do this?

After breakfast in the lodge, we met outside and sized up the weather. Roberto geared up, put on his impressive sunglasses with the blinders on the sides, and said, "Listo?" I nodded, smiled, and threw on my fancy pack—for the very first time.

I'd been so preoccupied with training for the distance that

it never occurred to me to train for the weight. I assumed if I had done the mileage, a pack wouldn't be a problem. I was a fool. Forty pounds on your back and hiking uphill is like learning to walk again. I said nothing to Roberto, but I was freaking out. At a quarter of a mile, the waist pad from my pack was cutting so deep into my hips I thought I might have blisters. I'm capable "in the moment." Most of my life, I've improved by trial and error more than by advanced planning. This has the effect of making the initial round of something I do rough and not great, but it always gets better from there. For the first time in my life, I thought that my carelessness, my overconfidence, and my foolish optimism had taken me too far. I was at the bottom of the world, didn't speak Spanish, was out of my league, and had no business being there.

Two thoughts controlled my mind: "Don't stop" and "Don't think about the fact that this is still the flat." During our morning breakfast briefing, Roberto had introduced me to three Patagonia terms: "Flat," "Up," and a new term, "Patagonia Flat." The first two mean what you think: It's flat, it's up—very self-explanatory. Patagonia Flat is what large portions of the "W" were, stretches of incline followed by stretches of some decline before more incline. The net elevation increase ends up being small because the down cancels out the up, hence Patagonia Flat. I'd been told this morning, we'd be "Flat, Up Up Up," and then lots of good Patagonia Flat, before "really big Up Up Up." As the flat became the up, my legs went numb, and my childhood experiences hiking the Appalachian trail to Mount Katahdin kicked in. Good foot placement. Breathe. Use your arms. Don't stop. I was dying and convinced I couldn't go on, but I had to make it to the ridge to find a way to tell Roberto we had to turn back.

Around forty-five minutes into the hike, Roberto told me to stop for water by the sign. I was wrecked, posturing, and trying to hide my fear. I struggled to find an opening to drop the bad news that I couldn't go on. I smiled sideways at him and said, "Can I ask you something?" He grinned wide and, as if from a script, said, "Of course, I am not just pretty face!" I lost it. He has one of the best laughs, and both his words and his laugh caught me off guard. Trying to breathe, I asked about our pace. This would be my opening: "How are we doing?"

"*Muy bueno!* Most groups have to stop three times by now. We are very fast. I can tell in the first ten minutes if someone is trekker or not, or if they have too many office days to be able to climb. You a real trekker. Good feet. Strong. Not afraid to lead."

What?

I was stunned. I protested. No, no, we were slow. Yes, I was in front, but I was sure Roberto was being slowed by me. And besides, my pack was killing me. I told him I wasn't as good as he thought. He smiled, came up behind me, shifted, pulled and tugged about five straps, and like magic, the pain from my pack was gone. He grabbed his gear, pointed uphill and said, "Listo?" "Sí." I was ready. Not because it was easier. Not because I was different. I knew I was ready because he believed I was. We all need people in our lives that give us permission to be extraordinary. They see us when we can't see ourselves. They appreciate our ability and know what it can do before we know it ourselves. I borrowed Roberto's belief until I could find some of my own. I needed him to give me permission to be me.

## What Do You Believe?

I wish that understanding identity were enough. Through my company, almost 900 people a year take Clifton Strengths to understand their talent and purpose. In workshops, consulting sessions, and a variety of other formats, I'm asked to talk to individuals about their genius and the impact they can have on the world. That's close to 10,000 people over the last thirteen years that have completed a world-class assessment, received a customized Insight Guide, and got to hear someone talk about the validity of the results and where they can apply them. If understanding were enough, this army of 10,000—and the now over eighteen million global Clifton Strengths participants—would have transformed our world.

So why don't we? What are we afraid of? Why do we keep making excuses? When will we stop justifying our grip on safety? We will never quit limiting ourselves until we start to believe. We have to accept that our identity is worth following. The road you're carving can carry people to places they'd never go alone. The understanding you uncover will transform how we see ourselves and others. But do you believe it? Most people don't.

Human beings like hearing good things about themselves. They like the possibility of being great, but they think focusing on talent, purpose, and passion are all a soft-skill sales pitch with no actual power. But there's nothing soft about what I'm suggesting.

> *It's not enough for people to seek out an extraordinary life.*

People who understand their identity, move toward it, and are given opportunities to express it day to day live more emotionally engaged lives. The statistics show this engagement makes them more productive, thriving, less sick, less bigoted, and safer at work. Any Gallup study on emotional engagement and well-being will provide the details (Gallup State of the Global Workplace is a good place to start). But hearing all that, it's not enough for people to seek out an extraordinary life. They need permission.

# Did You Ask Permission?

People don't like the word *permission*. When I told friends that I was writing about the power of permission, their reactions weren't enthusiastic. The underlying sentiment was that people shouldn't need to ask anyone's permission to live their life! I agree, but many people still feel as though they do. Have you ever wondered why?

*Permission* comes from a similar root word as "to permit." To allow, consent, agree—these words all go with *permission*. I like metaphors, and as I was thinking about why people struggled to embrace their own compass, this came to mind.

In our modern world, you have to receive a building permit before you can begin construction. You have to tell the authorities what you want to do, what resources you have to make it happen, and the impact you'd like to have on the surrounding environment. They decide if you have everything you need to execute your plan. If you do, they give you a permit.

To prevent this from getting lost, you'll often find this permit in plastic taped to a window or wall of the construction site. In fact, you can get a fine if an inspector pulls ups and you don't have the permit posted. You always know where your permit is, and anytime some inspector or cranky neighbor tries to complain or stop you, you point to the permit and charge on.

This is how it was supposed to be. You're born. You have talents. You have passions. You start to dream. You begin to make plans. The relationships in your life—mother, father, siblings, your family of origin—they're supposed to give you your permit. They'll ask questions, push for examples, and at the end of the day, you get their endorsement: The stamp from the highest authority in your life. You keep it with you everywhere you go. And any time a bully, a critic, or a broken world tries to tell you you're foolish and can't have the impact you want, the permit from the source that matters shuts them down.

Too bad it doesn't happen like this.

*We are imperfect people raised by imperfect people.*

We are imperfect people raised by imperfect people. And parents not given a permit by their parents don't know how to give one to their children. So we go on without it. We grow up and begin to live but never feel like we have permission. We hope we do. We act like we do. We oversell our abilities. We learn never to show doubt, but we worry that people will discover we're frauds.

It's incredible the number of people who tell me that the world doesn't need permission—but everyday people make choices like they're frantic for it. It's becoming so familiar you can Google "imposter syndrome." There's an entire condition growing in our culture where people do not feel secure in the impact and success they're having in life, and they're convinced others are going to discover that they're imposters who have no permission to be doing what they're doing. If our identities are the true north of our compass, then permission is its south pole. It's the vision, the expression, the direction you'll find yourself in if you keep going north long enough.

## Nothing You Don't Already Know

I didn't recognize the human need for permission when I first started out. Like so many speakers and trainers, I still held on to the formula that information equals transformation. Share it, speak it, teach it, and as long as they are absorbing the material, change will occur. Too many in my profession still believe this. We want to. It's dependable. It's neat. It's clean. I give you information.

You take it. You become transformed. It's all about you. All I do is deliver. I wanted this to be true. But as my clients spent year after year in the same place, it wasn't working.

Looking back, my own imposter syndrome blinded me. I was insecure. I didn't want to get too involved. I was the king of Clifton Strengths workshops. I'd tell the jokes, drive the point, and wrap it up with as close to an altar call as most people had ever heard. People would laugh, cry, and go through all the emotions. They'd line up afterward to ask me questions. I'd tell them about their themes and impress them with the bizarre things their results translated to, but that's where I'd end. I wouldn't give advice. I didn't want the pressure.

Over time, I got more corporate clients. I still did the show, as I called it, but now they'd ask me to meet for dinner for debriefing. The debriefs started to sound the same. "Mike, this is great information, but we want to change our department. What do you think we should do?" Each time I would respond by saying, "Look, Clifton Strengths themes are descriptive, not prescriptive. It's a tool. You know your industry best. I'm a teacher, not a consultant. Good luck!" That was my script for years until the night they wouldn't let me off the hook.

I did a workshop with one of my regular clients and her team. We went out to dinner, and we were talking about all the changes she believed were needed: reorganizing her department, workflow, staffing, positions—everything. She understood the problems and had a grasp of her resources, and she laid out her plan. Finishing her summary, she paused and asked me, "What do you think?" I rolled out my auto-reply: ... you're the expert ... it's a profile ... themes describe ... blah, blah, blah. Frustrated, she reacted, "Mike, I've paid you thousands of dollars for this day. I've purchased the right to hear your opinion. What do you think?"

Surprised, I took a breath and said the first things that came to mind. I agreed with her challenges. She understood her people. She might want to keep an eye out on some unseen problems, but I thought she was on track. My words were not exceptional; they were an echo of hers. I agreed with her, and so I said so.

Months later, they had more growth and more change than in the past year of my working with them. When I asked about the impetus for the change, they said they already knew what was right and what they wanted to do, but my words gave them permission to go ahead and do it.

I had found a key for personal transformation. People didn't need perfect information or the newest plan on the street. They were looking for a person who could say, "I see you. You're not alone. I'm not scared, and we can walk this road together." They wanted someone to give them permission to be the person or team that they believed in their heart they were.

There's a world-changing power created when a person's belief in their identity meets a relationship of permission. The insecure becomes dependable, the theoretical becomes a reality, and the fearful Patagonian rookie finds a way to climb it all. Five more times, in fact.

# 9

# AUTHORITY

To punish me for my contempt for authority,
fate made me an authority myself.
—*Albert Einstein*

When I was twelve years old, I began working at Cedar Valley Farm. Homesteaded near the turn of the century, it was the last farm at the end of Happy Corner Road. That's the actual road name, by the way. What started as a few afternoons throwing hay bales became gutter cleaning, mending fences, herding cows, and whatever chores needed to be done on the 1,000-acre dairy farm. Any mechanical ability I have today came from ten years working at Cedar Valley. It was hard and demanding, but those were some of the most satisfying days of my life.

Farm work is a catalyzer accelerating childhood maturity. Working there, I experienced trust but also expectation. I had to pull my weight, which meant I learned to drive a car at age twelve and to drive a stick shift by the time I was thirteen. Underage driving was a rite of passage, and the farmer, Robert Guptill, would let me drive his pickup the mile from the barn to the house when we'd go home for breakfast or dinner. Of the hundreds of times I made the drive over the years, one night stands out.

My dad came to pick me up from the farmhouse. Robert wanted to show him some welding back at the barn. We hopped in the pickup to make the one-mile drive before sunset. It was a beautiful summer night, so my dad sat down on the tailgate of the pickup for the ride over. But after walking to the truck, Robert got in on the passenger side and gave me the "you're driving" look. Split-second fear is still fear. I was a kid who had never driven his dad anywhere, and now I was driving him to the barn in the GMC truck with the stick.

I started the engine. Robert looked at me, smiled, and said, "Breathe. You can do this. Nice and easy." I eased out the clutch, and we glided away down the pothole-patched road. My dad never said a word, but smiled.

That moment of wrestling with confidence to believe I was becoming a man was possible because Robert gave me permission to be one. Much like Roberto years later, I borrowed his belief until I got my own. But what made him believable? Vision results from permission, but you can't have permission without relationships you give authority. I trusted Robert, and if he was trustworthy all the other times in my life, I had to trust him when he said I was a man. Authority is the root of permission.

## Permission Begins at Home

In a perfect world, we would get the bulk of our "permit" or permission from our core relationships: our families of origin. They would encourage us, support us, and call out potential we didn't know we had. They'd validate our ideas, empathize with our pain, and when we went out on a limb, they would climb out there with us. Family is supposed to be strong and wise, and so we give them authority to shape us. This original system of familial relationships and permission is compelling, and when it works, it produces compelling results.

When I was a freshman in high school, my little brother David came home one night and told me Jake, a kid in his sixth-grade class, was bullying him. He'd made fun of something he'd done. As kids, David and I were never allies, but I had a burning hatred for bullies. I never wanted anyone to have to go through my bullying, even if he was my brother. Truth be told, it was because he was my brother.

I was angry for him in a way I never was before. I had to have his back. I wouldn't let this slide.

The next morning, I skipped the first period and walked across the street to the junior high. My reputation as Mr. Nice Guy allowed me to knock on this kid's homeroom door and interrupt his class. I told the teacher I needed to see Jake. "It will be quick," I promised. I can't believe she let me pull him into the hallway, but Jake came shuffling out. And as the door closed, I got up in his face.

He'd been talking crap about my brother. I had heard. It was going to stop. If it didn't end, there would be consequences. Wide-eyed, he apologized and said it would never happen again. He was motivated by my imposing demeanor and intimidating presence. Well, actually, not so much. It was more likely the muscled friend I brought with me.

My brief career as a gangster was about me on some level, but at its core, it was about David. He was my brother; he was a part of me. His pain lit a fire in me to not have someone steal my brother's confidence away. On a primal level, it felt right that I should be the one to stand up for him. But one supportive moment doesn't replace a thousand others. In many ways I used my authority as his big brother to contribute to David's bank of permission, endorsement, and encouragement over the first twenty years of his life, but I made lots of withdrawals too. More than I want to admit. Like many of us, he would have to go find his missing permission somewhere else.

# It Takes a Village

You know the saying, "It takes a village." When it comes to permission, it's true. For the first twenty-two years of life, our mind is a running balance sheet of deposits and withdrawals. It takes a village of relationships to keep the books balanced.

Robert Guptill encouraging me to drive: *deposit.*

Fired by Mr. C. for talking too much: *withdrawal.*

Mocked by teachers in junior high: *withdrawal.*

Mrs. Ellis coming out from the grocery store with the sole purpose of telling me I made a great stop (my only stop) in the soccer game: *deposit.*

Like an accounting register of permission, transactions continue to accumulate until around the age of twenty-two when something unexpected happens. The Massachusetts Institute of Technology (MIT) Young Adult Development Project captures fascinating facts about the young adult brain and prefrontal cortex development. This area of the brain is just behind our foreheads and is responsible for what MIT calls the "executive suite." This includes decision-making, long-term planning, risk and reward analysis, and self-governing behavior. Surprisingly, this part of the brain is not completely connected to the rest of the brain until our mid twenties. This provides the answer as we look back on our freshman year of college and ask, "What were we thinking?" The scientific response is that we weren't thinking. We are heavily shaped by others, but after this brain connection is solidified, we begin to think for ourselves.

The essential thing to know is that as we graduate high school and move into our twenties, the books are closed, the profits are counted, and our amount of existing permission is tabulated. And with that, we go out into the world. It's stable, it can be drafted on, it's dependable in day-to-day life. But if that's the case, think back to age twenty-two. What was your final balance?

Did you finish in the black? Did you have the emotional support and clarity you needed to develop a vision for your life? Was it enough then? Is it enough now? Has your growing understanding revealed a deficit you didn't know you had? Do you feel confident enough to dream of a successful job but lack the confidence to build a business? Do you feel you have the permission you need to move toward your identity and not live trapped by circumstance and stuck in someone else's rut?

If, as my grandmother liked to say, your cup runneth over, great. You can skip the rest of this chapter. But if you realize your life is going places you never imagined, or if you're aware of a permission deficit that is holding you back day to day, then we're going to need to top off your balance.

## You're Not the Boss of Me!

In Dr. Henry Cloud's book *Boundaries for Kids*, he talks about children being boundaryless. They pour themselves into the containers that parents create for them. I believe that continues into adolescence when the boundaries of our lives shift to our peers and friends. These people in proximity are the deposits and debits of our permission to be us. Our relational control at this age is pretty limited. Without tools, we let people give and take from us emotionally without much ability to stop them. Our parents and the community we grow up in have a massive impact on the level of endorsement we operate in after the age of twenty-two. But if we have little control as children, we have the opposite as adults.

As kids, important relationships were a dime a dozen. The popular kid in class, the actor on a sitcom, or the musician on our sibling's wall—it didn't take much to believe their opinions mattered. This is why the old parenting retort to bullied kids of "sticks and stones may break my bones but words will never hurt me" is complete garbage. That saying may be accurate, or at least more accurate after my early twenties when my developing self begins to realize not every voice matters. But when we're young, we have an active "permissional economy," and every interaction gives or takes. As adults, we need different tactics.

After our twenties, the only way to bolster a sense of permission is through intentional relationships. More specifically, relationships that we give authority. This is our challenge. We're conditioned as adults to yield authority to no one other than ourselves. We're led to believe that to let others have a voice of authority in our lives is to be incompetent. To be accountable is to be restrained. Nobody wants a boss. But there's no way to cultivate permission in our lives if we don't have relationships that can be there for us with an endorsement. We need mentors, pastors, coaches, therapists, and any connections that have the substance worthy of putting our dreams into their hands. This is an intentional process in an unintentional world.

## Intentional Relationship

Genuine, life-changing permission comes from cultivated relationships of authority. You have to seek out people that you can trust. People who have experience wrestling with understanding their identity. You're looking for people who've dreamed and failed and dreamed again. You want individuals who make hard choices and understand sacrifice. And you want to surround yourself with people who help you see a world bigger than yourself. The fruit of these connections are the sources of permission and vision in your own life. But you've got to nurture them, invite them into your life, and then give them authority to make deposits into your life.

Counterfeit permission is easier to come by. You can find it from everywhere, and it's usually permission to be self-destructive. Social media, television, and advertising all thrive on showing you your faults, promising you a future, and justifying any choice to fill the gap. We believe them not because of the content of their character but by their number of followers and relevance of their newsfeed. The entire concept of social media influencers is based on this idea. More than one billion dollars a year is paid to people online to convince others that they should buy, use, or pursue something because this person tells them to. And according to the government, 90 percent of social media audiences have no idea they're being sold.

The key to gathering the relationships of permission is to treat your time with people like a resource to manage. Spend thoughts and feelings on people who are worthy of returning of the investment.

> *The people and information we allow into our lives will set our course for years to come.*

Who are your friends? Are you selective about who you let into your life and the voices you listen to? I once had a mentor named Frank who loved to say, "Show me a man's friends and the books he reads, and I'll show you who he'll be in five years." He's right. The people and information we allow into our lives will set our course for years to come.

I was blessed to have a Robert in my childhood before I became a man. Today, I hope to be that man for others.

# 10

# VISION

The only thing worse than being blind
is having sight and no vision.
—*Helen Keller*

My friend Nick Webb is a brilliant British gentleman. He's always ready with a fascinating story, a great question, or a joke that is almost always over my head. I love visiting with him and his wife Jan, and I've enjoyed their hospitality on multiple holiday visits. A few things about Nick stand out. He's generous, sacrificial, and does nothing halfway. One year during a stay with his family in Wales, he heard me say I'd love to visit Ireland sometime. Forty-eight hours later, we were on the ten o'clock morning express ferry (two and a half hours) across the raging Irish Sea to Dublin. We'd have time to squeeze in a quick tour of the city before racing to catch the eight o'clock ferry (four hours) back to Wales so we could catch our train to London the next day. The man does nothing halfway.

After a taxi to the city center, we decided the Big Red Bus was our best option to get around, and off we went. It was a blast. Halfway through the tour loop, we came to the famous Guinness Brewery. My first beer had been a Guinness. I loved it but knew nothing about the company. Deciding we wanted to do more than see sights from a bus window on our spontaneous adventure, we hopped off and went in for the tour. It was something I'll never forget.

A state-of-the-art facility, this was a multisensory experience. I walked through the story of brewing, the process, the company, and its legacy. There were walls of waterfalls to show the importance of water, and I ran my hand through bins of hops and grain. It was more experience than tour. But it was the history that moved me most.

Under glass in the entrance lobby floor is the original lease from 1759 requested and signed by Arthur Guinness. He gathered all the money he could and leased the run-down brewery at the mouth of the St. James River. It was a bit of a fool's errand, but he was determined to make it go. When asked by the landlord what terms he wanted in the lease, he said 9,000 years. Let that sink in: 9,000 years. Call it hubris or vision—either way, I love it.

Throughout the tour, there were comments about how much Guinness valued his employees. This was proved when the staff of coppersmiths, who handmade oak kegs, were on the verge of being unemployed as the industry shifted to steel. Instead of laying off the staff, whose skills were no longer needed, the company employed the woodworkers to craft and produce oak furniture. When the last coppersmith died, the furniture was discontinued.

Both fascinated by the hints of a bigger story than beer brewing, as Nick and I said our goodbyes that weekend, he presented me the book *Searching for God and Guinness* by Stephen Mansfield. Mansfield had researched Arthur Guinness, and what he found was an incredible story of vision by an entrepreneur at a time when the world needed it most.

In a day when your options for quenching your thirst were whiskey, gin, or the poisonous river water, beer was a lifesaver. An experienced brewer, Arthur turned the old brewery into a success and began amassing a significant family fortune. But Guinness was unsatisfied until his life was transformed by a traveling preacher.

In the late 1700s, John Wesley, the famous teacher of socially responsible faith, came to Dublin to speak at St. Patrick's. Guinness was fascinated by this man who was known for telling congregations "Make all you can, save all you can, and give all you can." Arthur found a new vision for his life, and he lived it radically. He was determined to make Guinness one of the most significant forces for good in the world.

The largest employer in Dublin, Guinness paid 20 percent more than anyone else. Since employees didn't have time to go see doctors, he hired them and built clinics onsite. The company constructed employee housing, offered low-cost home loans for those who wanted to buy their own houses, and believed it was wrong to use people to improve the company if they didn't improve employees' lives too.

This culture was influential, and it endured for hundreds of years. According to Mansfield, by 1928, the year before the Great Depression, Guinness employees had free, twenty-four-hour medical care, dental care, and onsite massage therapy. Funeral costs were free, employees received a no-contribution pension and education for all dependent children, and spouses were paid by the Guinness company. The employees had libraries, reading rooms, and athletic facilities and were given all-expenses-paid trips to the countryside each year. One person's vision of an extraordinary life transformed the lives of generations.

What do you see?

We've talked about identity, and maybe you are starting to believe. Maybe you're taking your stock of permission and seeking the investment of more relationships. But you will know you're living with permission when your identity shapes the things you see. When it comes to the relationship between vision and permission, it's both correlation and causation. Having people give permission helps free you to see a different future, but working to craft a vision for your life will help give you permission to believe in what your identity says is true. The litmus test of permission is whether you have a vision.

> *The litmus test of permission is whether you have a vision.*

The evidence of permission is the presence of a dream. If I meet talented people who have done the research on themselves but are still asking others what they should be, I know they suffer from a lack of permission. People who have been endorsed and encouraged become curious. Like a toddler prompted to walk, once they do, they almost never stop. It's a snowball building on itself. But it has to start somewhere, and that somewhere is always a relationship of authority.

While the result of permission is a growing vision, the reverse can also be true. Permission is a lot like a muscle: It atrophies without use. I look for vision in others as a barometer of their level of permission, but the best way to develop a sense of endorsement is making an effort to dream. We need to practice. We need to take out our driver's license and go for a spin. Get out around the block. Then hit the other side of town. Before you know it, you're planning a road trip you never thought you'd make. But you've got to believe you can.

What I love about the story of Arthur Guinness is that he knew who he was. He had found a purpose for his talents and a 9,000-year passion for his endeavors, but neither were enough. It took a relationship with a minister, or better said, his relationship with his God to spark the vision that would transform his life. A sermon became an idea that became a choice. That became practice, that became a policy, that became a movement that shaped a nation. But it started with a glimpse of a vision of a life lived for more.

So, what's the plan?

This vision that's rooted in permission and anchored to our identity is key to navigation toward you. Having sight on the path you're traveling to get where you're going will impact all your plans. During sessions, I'll tell clients they're participating in a race and they can have any vehicle they want. People offer up their favorite sports car and explain the attributes. Porsche engines have insane turbo, Ferraris are Ferraris, but Teslas have a geared transmission unlike anything on the market. Then I tell them the race is through a field up the side of a hill. They all groan. Clarifying the conditions of the course changes the vision of what's needed. Permission that sparks or clarifies vision is about more than inspiration. Vision clarifies planning. And you can't navigate without a plan. Here's some of the road conditions you need to keep in mind as you craft your vision.

## Dreams

As I've already mentioned, the first sign of permission is the presence of a dream. I'm not talking about the weird dreams where your teeth fall out, or you're supposed to give an unprepared speech in front of hundreds. Dreams are thoughts and hopes about your future, your legacy, or something you could engage in that would bring life to you and others. People with permission first permit themselves to dream and to envision a better or more fulfilling life. They spend mental energy considering what is possible and don't consider it a luxury or waste. The common phrase running on the train track in their mind is "What if I ... ?"

Are you dreaming? Are you out of practice? There are a few seasons when dreaming is considered acceptable: high school, college, first job, midlife crisis, first retirement, final retirement. Other than those moments and all the days in between, people tell you to put your head down so you can watch your feet and march on. Be careful—don't fall out of the rut.

> *Do you have a dream you haven't dared share?*

Are you dreaming? Do you and your spouse dream? Do you remember how? Do you have a dream you haven't dared share? Find the trusted relationships that can provide a judgment-free place to propose your vision and dreams. Make it a practice.

## Risks

The second indicator of a life of permission is a growing tolerance of risk. Permission makes us see our dreams as more than child's play, which means they have power, but there will be a cost. You know you've moved beyond the ideas of identity and permission when you begin considering the cost of a choice. People who don't have permission don't risk. They see the world as a zero-sum game, and any direction that requires uncertainty can never return its investment or price.

How's your tolerance for risk? What ideas are you stopping before they even start? When was the last time you invested time, money, or credibility in something that wasn't a sure thing? When you have a balance of permission, you know that any loss can never diminish the value of you. Vision shaped by identity is at least worth considering the risk.

## Failure

People who live with permission don't always get it right. The risks they take don't always work. Put another way, sometimes they fail. A person with permission is allowed to fail because failure is part of the journey toward the dream. Lack of failure isn't a measure of an idea's worthiness. You'll never live freely from the circumstances of your life if you think your plans can never fail. A mistake can be corrected, but a missed opportunity is gone forever. Fail faster. Don't be afraid. As I shared in early pages, you have to try things on to find a purpose fit. Some of these trials will fail. Remember that you're living a life of things you "get to do," not "have to do." You are not your failure, though it's a part of your story. For lives lived with permission, the steps after defeat are the most impactful. Don't fear failure.

## Growth

The last piece of permission is growth. People who are doing things they believe they're made to do see every moment as a chance to be transformed. Everything can be used to clarify, shape, or align their journey. The growth that comes from permission is from the posture of anticipation. Anticipation opens us up in simple but profound ways.

What if I told you tomorrow you'd meet an individual that would change your life? How would you wake up in the morning? How would you look at people you pass on the street? As the hours go by, what would happen to your excitement? When you believe in your potential, you will make choices for yourself, and your life will be changed. You look at problems in new ways, seeing moments as lessons and wonder how each interaction can create personal growth.

Dreams, risk, failure, and growth are like signposts on the road that tell you that you're moving in the right direction. Don't avoid them. Living extraordinary lives can be messy. And the scars of disaster to others are trophies of triumph that we'll show loved ones one day. You'll tell the story how, like Arthur, you didn't dream in years, you dreamed in millennia. You were strong, and you knew it, but you wanted to be strong for others. And you'll tell how you listened to the chorus of permission as the wise sent you out and welcomed you home after accomplishing what others dared not do. The next two chapters are stories of people who had a vision of their world bigger than themselves. They deeply understood that there's a great power in permission.

# 11

# POWER OF PERMISSION

My father gave me the greatest gift anyone could
give another person: he believed in me.

—*Jim Valvano*

There's a power in permission. The lives of those who were foun-
dationally endorsed and taught to believe in the talent inside
themselves leave a mark on the world. In business, education, and
community, people who think they have something to give—do,
and everyone around them is better for it.

I've had the honor of being a mentor and friend to the partners of the Moniker Group in San Diego for years. If you ask them
who they are, their answer might surprise you.

We're a family of doers, builders, self-starters, innovators, and
story makers. We're founded and grounded in enabling people to
accomplish what they didn't think possible.

We invest in people and brands to build dreams and
experiences.

We hope to see a world dramatically impacted by people who
are working in their gifts and talents to create environments for
others to connect, be inspired, grow, and take action toward their
dreams.

Do you know what they do? Well, they do events, furniture, design, real estate, co-working space, retail, and run one of the hottest new cocktail bars in San Diego. Founded by Ryan Sission, whose courage and charisma could fill a chapter alone, Moniker took on partners in 2016 as the company vision expanded. One of those partners was an entrepreneur named Nathan Cadieux.

Because he's the president of Real Estate for Moniker Group, I wanted to know what it takes to leave an impressive tenure at one of the most successful companies in San Diego to strike out on his own on this dream that became Moniker Real Estate. Planning, investors, design, retail, restaurants, and city politics in the high-wire world of Southern California real estate—how does a guy not yet thirty-five find the courage to believe in the vision he saw? Here's what he had to say.

## Nate

I've never felt like I wanted to "follow the pack" or do what was right in the eyes of others. I wanted more out of life. I wanted it to be an adventure, thrilling, exciting, and always new. I grew up in a home that was always changing, whether it was family dynamics, moving, or going to different schools. Because of that, I thrive on change more than consistency.

After earning my business degree, I got my first job in real estate and quickly knew I'd eventually chart my own course. But I live by the idea that I needed to "earn the right" to share the best of me. Choosing to walk your own path, whether as an entrepreneur, in your career, or your industry, doesn't happen overnight. You need to develop experience, relationships, and credibility. You need to refine your talent, and that often occurs while working for someone else.

For six years at McMillin Companies, I showed up ready to work to help the company accomplish its goals. I did what I was asked to do to the best of my abilities, I was responsible, and I was always willing to take on more wherever I could. This gave me opportunities to learn and grow. It took me four years to "earn the right" to be invited into the room to help solve the company's most significant problems.

I don't think you have to be an entrepreneur to live an extraordinary life, but it's been the path for me. I think there are plenty of companies led by exceptional people who would love to see their people reach their full potential. But when you feel like your beliefs and ideas have outgrown the position you're in, you have to ask hard questions. You need to consider the path that is best for you.

Having the courage to make the hard choices comes from cultivating our vision. We are what we eat, and we become what we tell ourselves. I was raised by a family · who believed I could become anything I wanted to be. It was never in an entitled "you're special" way but in the "stop complaining and go make something happen" way. I hear the voice of my family in my head a lot. Accept the crap life throws at you and don't sit in self-pity for more than a healthy amount of time. To live a life out of the ordinary, we have to be aware of our self-talk. We can be our own biggest hurdle to achieving the things we most deeply desire. Being kind to yourself is harder than we like to admit.

The other key to an extraordinary life is our relationships. I knew I needed to surround myself with people I could learn from. I sought out individuals who had achieved the success I hoped to find. They often inspired me, but they also permitted me to be human. They were imperfect, had a dream, took risks, and were doing the best with what they had. Those relationships gave me permission to start to dream and not worry about what I was not. It's so easy to think everyone else has something you don't. There's power in realizing that, in the beginning, everyone has to Google it.

If I look back at the relationships that were key for my belief in what is possible, it was my mom. Maybe everyone's mom believes in them, but mine was the foundation and model of a healthy relationship for me. So as I began working with others, I knew what an affirming relationship looked like and recognized the people who wanted to invest in me and see me become the best version of myself. I think we are all looking for someone to call our name; we might not always get it, but I was fortunate to have people around me who reminded me that it is always my turn, and I always had a choice.

Once you start down your own path in business, career, or your personal life, you have to manage the challenges and fears that would derail you. I'm learning to remind myself that our team can figure anything out. Too often, we believe that we can "get it right" if we just work, plan, push, or whatever. It's a myth. No one gets it 100 percent right. But if you can get 60 percent, then maybe over the next four months you can get 10 percent more right each month—all while getting to do the thing you love. Then a bit more and a bit more. It's progress, not perfection.

I'm trying to live by the belief that I am not my ability to be perfect and that together with my team, we can figure things out. This helps me stay grounded and feeling like I get to drive this life; it doesn't have to drive me.

> *Visualize yourself being efficient
> and successful today.*

If I could encourage people with anything, it's to keep your cause in front of you. You need a constant sight line to why you're taking a risk. Understanding and focusing on who and what motivates you is critical to starting on this road, but it's also critical to finishing it. Envision the future you want, and it will keep you from moping around feeling sorry for yourself when it gets hard. I like to find an encouraging word for myself every day. I have a quote in my priority notebook that says "Visualize yourself being efficient and successful today. You can overcome all obstacles." This keeps my head up, looking to the future of what can be instead of the barrier in front of me.

## Different Names, the Same Truth

I'm in awe of so many of my clients. They've dreamed and created remarkable things.

While each has a story to tell, there are core truths that are the same. As you listen to Nate's thoughts on his journey, you can hear them.

He had an internal vision of the life he wanted to lead. He was taught hard work and knew resilience would be required. He looked for relationships that would help him mature his perceptions and support his choices. He sacrificed. And when the time was right, he took a risk and started Moniker Real Estate with the Moniker team. But it all began with his mom.

The chain reaction of his identity sparked a relationship of permission that started the engine that powered his life. And this chain reaction keeps occurring.

As Nate points out the milestones on his journey to set his own professional course, note that those are not one-time events. Many successful people you meet will keep using the tools that work for them. Nate and Ryan continue to dream. Their search for new ways to express the identity of Moniker is constant. They lean heavily on their relationships, and they are intentional in seeking wise counsel. If you look around, you'll see the model repeated over and over in people who are impacting their world.

## Are You a Source of Permission?

If permission is the funding we need to begin to live out our vision of not following an ordinary life, the source is trustworthy relationships. I've focused on our need to cultivate these relationships, but my final question is this: Are you a source of permission for others? Back to our building permit analogy, are you helping people clarify their passion and talents? Are you helping them translate that into plans? Are you endorsing wise sacrificial risk? Are you committing not just to walk in front of people but alongside them?

*Gathering up permission empowers you;*
*giving it away empowers a community.*
*Permission creates innovation.*

Gathering up permission empowers you; giving it away empowers a community. Permission creates innovation.

We need to become venture capitalists of permission. If you've cultivated healthy relationships, you have a robust account. And like a venture capital firm, none of that capital will grow if we don't invest in outside ventures.

Who are the talented people that need to hear your voice? Are you someone who lets others take a risk? Do you allow people to engage you when you know they're looking for wisdom, and they see you as a mentor? Or are you too busy? Do your own dreams occupy all your time?

Those stingy with permission cheat themselves out of innovation. Invention is creation of something that never was. Innovation is a new application for things that already exist. Bosses who give permission inspire teams that take the past and create a future. Dads who let their sons become more than they are craft a legacy that will one day outlive them. And friends who are the voice of the positive and possible for the people in their lives discover great resource in times of need.

Nate would never have become the husband, entrepreneur, and leader he is if he hadn't had a mother who understood, gave him permission, and cheered him on the way. He sounds a lot like my friend in the next chapter who gathered a group of people to try to poke the universe.

# 12

# PERMISSION TO POKE THE UNIVERSE

*Who gave fire permission to burn?*

—*Marty Rubin*

All anyone wanted to ask was if I heard what the CEO said to the board. I had not, but by the fourth person, I could recite the gossip by memory. The story was he'd walked in, given a recap of his sabbatical residency at Stanford School of Design, thanked the board for their support, and told them he was done doing "junk" that didn't matter. My longest-standing client and good friend Michael Brennan had walked in and reset the world. You could feel the organization's collective heart skip a beat.

*He was done doing junk that didn't matter.*

I'm sure whatever he actually said was gracious but direct, as was his style. Brennan always could craft a dream of change that moved people. You don't raise over $700 million by not having vision. But there was something different about him now.

That day in the board meeting was the beginning of the end for Michael—the end of spending his life on things that did not move him.

What if your talents and passion have collided to create a vision so big that, even with all the balance in your permission account, you need more? If you're the founders of Civilla, you begin the search for lost tribe members. And like refugees from a world stuck in an echo chamber, once gathered around a mission, you change the world together.

Civilla, from the combination of the words *civil* (the role of citizens in a civil society) and *village* (based on the truth that nothing has ever been accomplished alone), is a design studio focused on change work.

In their own words:

> At the heart of Civilla is a family that wakes up every day to take action. We are a small community of leaders, designers, storytellers, artists, urbanists, social work- ers, technologists, and troublemakers who have come together in support of Civilla's mission and purpose.
>
> We are on a mission to change the way that "change- work" happens. In the United States, we have billions of dollars that flow into services every year without signifi- cant changes in the quality of life for residents. At Civilla, we wake up every day asking ourselves: How do we find a new way forward so that the way things are does not become the way things will always be?
>
> Each week we re-dedicate ourselves to a ten-year walk to poke the universe. We'll know that we've achieved this when we have positively impacted one billion people and deeply impacted one thousand lives. It's also why we named our podcast *One Billion*. There is no way we will be

able to do this alone. It will take a community of leaders and change makers to rally around a new way forward.

"To poke the universe." I love that. I'm not sure what it means, but it feels significant and audacious, and it seems even more so when you realize it started in a gutted room in the heart of Detroit with no heat, ceiling, or anything that's supposed to matter. All they needed was a dream and each other.

As I worked on this chapter, I decided Michael would be a great interview about how the relationships in his life gave him permission to start Civilla. It didn't go the way I planned.

I asked him where he found the permission to leave the prestige of a life in nonprofit service to go off on his own.

## Michael

Permission was granted by myself and came to me from a place of internal pain. No outside individual could have granted me the permission to leave my job of thirty-two years because no outside individual was forcing me to stay. After taking a three-month leave from my role as CEO of a large nonprofit in Detroit, I made a promise to myself. I said that I would never again "squint to see myself." During the three months away, I realized that I had gotten far from who I was and what I was meant to do. Six months after my return from the sabbatical, I found myself once again "squinting to see myself." That is, I was responding to the external forces versus being driven by the purpose of my life. That gap contained such a peak level of dissonance that I knew I had to take action. I walked downstairs and said to my wife that I was going to announce to my board leadership that it was time for me to leave the organization and for the organization to prepare for its next leader. I had no idea what I was going to do next, but I was confident in the decision.

Trying to work my permission angle, I asked Michael another question. "What part did permission play in navigating this new road?"

The permission I granted to myself helped me step into the unknown. I had in my previous role a very defined and public role. I announced my departure without clarity on what would be next for myself and how I would make a living. The level of uncertainty and ambiguity was scary but thrilling. I knew if I stayed in the role I had been in, it would have been dangerous to my health, soul, and psyche. I knew at my core that the permission to step into the unknown would be scary but not dangerous. I chose scary.

I gave my permission hook one more try: "Now that you live this scary but thrilling mission to 'poke the universe,' what part does permission play?"

If you imagine changing the world and "poking the universe," then waiting for the permission truck to roll up to your front door and unload unlimited permission slips is a hallucination. I have found granting myself the permission to step into the life and work I imagined requires constant attention. There is no magic permission pill to take. The amount of permission you grant yourself is in direct correlation to how much work you do in the acceptance of self. The more I understand that, the more likely we can discover what the full expression of ourselves looks like in this vast cosmic universe.

I love this man. Even when he doesn't answer the way I script, he still helps me out. Michael is still making my point: Permission is vital, permission creates vision, permission grows from relationships—and the most critical permission relationship is with yourself.

## Check the Balance

In the majority of this section, I've focused on trying to solve the problem of how a lack of emotional support can prevent us from stepping toward our identities, or as Michael put it, the life we imagine. This is a real problem, and I wanted to address it. You need to start with awareness of what your starting adult permission balance is. You need to decide if that's enough permission to get you where you need to go. To develop more, you have to cultivate relationships with authority that can resource your dreams. But the most critical relationship of authority is the one you have with you. This is what Michael is saying.

There's no doubt that Michael's father instilled a sense of strength and capability in his children after the passing of his mother. The reliable partnership he experiences with his wife Joan is a constant reservoir of encouragement. And the community he encountered for a short season at Stanford and now in the Civilla family is a resource that he can't do without. But at the end of the day, he has to sign the check alone.

Ever know someone who acts like they're broke all the time? They analyze the restaurant bill to make sure they don't get charged for an extra soda. They never offer to treat. They're afraid and always worried about what they don't have. And then you find out they're rich. This describes too many of us. Don't be cheap, in particular with yourself.

More people may have held you back than endorsed you when you were young. You haven't always been clear about your talents. And from time to time, you've given people voice in your life that you should have ignored. But I'll bet you're not as "broke" as you think. Check your balance, think about the people who believe in you. Make a list of the things that have gone right and point in the direction of the life you imagine. Find your answer to what you think your life should look like and decide because no one else can. You have to start, you have to take action, you have to move. Or it's all a waste.

This is a problem in our world. We're starting to become aware of the years of naysayers and restrictions. The way we've held people back. We're seeing the price of penalizing people who didn't fit our mold. The good news is that it's producing a push on permission. Look at famous sites and newsfeeds. They're all chanting, "Speak your truth!" Great, but then what?

It doesn't matter if you've gathered the permission of the world but withhold it from yourself. Much like your identity, you have to believe. You have to do the work.

You need to gather permission. You need to protect it. But you also need to spend it. No one else can poke the universe exactly like you can. And that takes courage. And that's where we're headed next.

# Part 3

# COURAGE:
# How Will You
# Get There?

# 13

# DEFINING COURAGE

Respect cannot be inherited;
respect is the result of right actions.

—*Amit Kalantri*

In 2015, I was on a small prop plane flying from Seattle, Washington, to Edmonton, Alberta. Losing the seatmate lottery, I ended up in 4A and, much to both our joys, a guy larger than me was in 4B. As he settled in, we made our mutual apologies and clicked our seat belts for the two-hour flight across the Canadian Rockies. As we taxied to the end of the runway, the tapping began.

His cupped right hand started tapping his thigh like a metronome. My first thought was obsessive-compulsive disorder. It was measured like he was counting. I thought it odd but waved it off as he nodded off while the plane was holding on the tarmac. And then, as we began to lift off, something dropped from his hand. He woke, and after fumbling for what had fallen, the tapping started again.

I tried not to stare, but I couldn't look away. That's when I saw it. My seatmate would tap, tap, tap, then turn over his hand and look at his palm. It was a pedometer. He was faking steps!

He did this the entire flight. I was cracking up. I imagined his hotel phone call with his wife that night explaining that he treated himself to the cheesecake. "But, honey, I walked hard today; I've got the pedometer to prove it." This is our problem. We've gotten so far off track that we fake the signs of effort. We want the rights that come with action but without the sacrifice. We cultivate justifications for our demands instead of taking actions to earn them. We want the cheesecake but not the effort that would make the cheesecake an actual reward. Unfortunately, there is no courage without action, so courage can't be faked.

## How Did We Get Here?

If *identity* is about accurately ascertaining where we are and *permission* is about vision and planning to get where we want to go, then *courage* is about the action required to go there. People aren't faking courage. They're right to want the rewards that come from acts of sacrifice and bravery, but they're confusing marks of courage for the thing itself. Throughout history, the courageous were afforded privileges, and to convey those rights, they were often given symbols. Today we call them status symbols.

In ancient times, communicating wasn't easy. Illiteracy, no printing press, no mass media. Civilization was an oral culture. Education, history, and current events were passed down in conversations and memorialized in stories. To share significant or momentous news, you had to tell it. If someone was brave, daring, or courageous, it had to be announced. Ancient kings had people whose jobs were to walk around before and behind them shouting their accolades. The Old Testament of the Bible tells the story of Haman from the Persian Empire who, wanting this for himself, was tricked into having to walk in front of his mortal enemy Mordecai shouting how great he was and how much the king loved him.

The Greeks and Romans did this too, but their resources brought in something new: symbols and icons. They loved art and illustration and had the funds to pay a craftsman to create representations communicating their significance. You could have your latest military conquest carved on a wall. Instead of needing "criers" following you, you cut the image once, and the people told the story. It was more explicit, more impressive, and had the added value of expressing your greatness after you were gone. Or at least until your successor had your head chopped off your sculptures.

The purview of the Greeks, symbols were powerful and engendered greatness more than storytelling. Icons were multi-sensory. One well-placed image could transform your reputation. But this was far too effective. People learned they could skip the act of courage and just paint the valiant picture. Icons and symbols, once an award of the courageous, became the property of the rich. But the value of the symbols remained.

In the Renaissance, it was typical for the emerging middle class to want to be seen as significant, despite their recent rise from the dust. You could pay artists from one of the famous schools in Italy to paint you into the virgin birth or some other critical moment. The Portinari Altarpiece includes the entire family hanging out with the angels and saints praying to the Virgin Mary. Until this altarpiece, people attempting prestige by association kept to the family looking on from the wings. But the Portinari piece put the kids beside the angels and Mary Magdalene looking over the shoulder of the favorite daughter. The family was sure this would ease their way into heaven.

Pendants, colors, titles—all created to communicate the courageous and sacrificial character of an individual—evolved into trophies to lord over people. They all start out so pure, but over time, they tell less about the individual the symbol is attached to and more about the society attaching it.

We still do this. Before World War II, buying a house was a symbol bestowed on those that achieved a level of success through hard work. Buying a home was the result of discipline and effort, and so homeownership became the symbol of the responsible and successful citizen. It's an enduring belief enough that owning your own home is still referred to as the American Dream. What does the proverb say about a dream deferred? It makes the heart sick.

Politicians didn't want to defer dreams. They needed people happy, and what better way than getting them a house? All you need is debt. Of course, your neighbors don't know that. They think you worked hard enough to get a house. The modern status symbol was born.

As access to capital increased through debt, so did the multiplication of status symbols in the late twentieth century. Houses, cars, families, vacations, titles, and the right social circle. The right purchase told the right story about you. Today, we post to our newsfeed, Snapchat, or Instagram story for the same reason. The more notice, the more our story is spread, the more people will value us. We've trained our culture to appreciate the fairytales. We craft courageous stories but not courageous lives.

*The Onion* is a satirical news website that posts ironic or satirical content. A favorite headline and photo from some years ago show a Caucasian, college freshman girl surrounded by children at an orphanage in Africa under the headline, "6-Day Visit to Rural African Village Completely Changes Woman's Facebook Profile Picture." Not her lesson in gratitude, not the mind-expanding experience of meeting people from a different context, she was thrilled about how photos of her with poor, nonwhite children were going to make her look to others. The clincher was the implication that everyone will be going there just as soon as they figure out how good it will be for their profile pics.

Fake article but real truth. We laugh at the story but still post "humble brags" on our pages.

"A busy day up here in first class working on my business plan, but this is just what it takes to be this successful."

"Hate when I have too many college acceptance letters."

"Here I am again, having to take my family to my mountain home in the Rockies. Hope you're having a good weekend wherever you are."

> *Social media isn't the problem—we are.*

We post things online that we would never say in person. Social media posts are like the Roman carved reliefs that could be created and left behind, letting the crowd draw their own conclusions. There is nothing wrong with sharing. I'm not anti-social media. I enjoy it and find it has made my brilliant international lifestyle so much easier to share with family and all my ever-loving fans. Just kidding.

Social media isn't the problem—we are.

## Where's a Good War When You Need One?

The problem with status symbols is that they are all about status, and status is all about where we stand. Social, professional, and relational status is about our ranking or position in comparison to something else. In history, if you weren't elite, the best way to change your situation or place in the community was courage and combat. In Lin-Manuel Miranda's cultural phenomenon *Hamilton*, the illegitimate, orphan immigrant Alexander Hamilton arrives in New York, escaping hurricane-ravaged Jamaica. After finding Aaron Burr and thinking he's discovered a kindred spirit, one as driven as he is, he says:

> You're an orphan. Of course! I'm an orphan
> God, I wish there was a war!
> Then we could prove we're worth more
> Than anyone bargained for.

Wishing for war was common in colonial times because it was the quickest way to elevate yourself. Being distinguished in war (or in marriage, and Hamilton did both) is how you got more opportunities. Well ... if you survived. In fact, in discussing General Mercer's legacy being complete because his name was on a new street, Burr says, "... and all he had to do was die. We should give it a try." Trying to get more out of life was accepted, but it was risky.

There was nothing wrong with ambition. There was nothing wrong with wanting to be more, but in the days of having a dream of a life outside the course of ordinary events, not bound to circumstance but navigating past them, their sole option was courageous action. The action produced renown, renown in society produced opportunity, and seized opportunity created a different life. Courageous acts distinguished the character of an individual. It set people apart from a preset notion of what they were capable of. Courageous actions told the outside world what was on the inside of a person. The symbols and stories were meant to spread that reputation. Change your view of this person: We've seen what they can do. They're worth more than anyone bargained for.

We continue to want to be more. We want to follow our paths. We want extraordinary lives. We don't want to live them, but we want to have them. We want to be special. We want to be separate. We want to be set apart. But we don't want to do the work that breaking free requires. And why would we want the pain involved in crafting a daring adventure when manufacturing the story of one is so much easier?

Besides, our world is ready with an infinite collection of status symbols packaged and prepared for you to express your uniqueness and significance.

Smartphones.

Headphones.

Job titles.

Addresses.

Sports team.

Car brands.

Your child's school.

Your political party.

Your child's volunteer work.

Pretty much anything your child does can be used to show you're an exceptional and courageous person.

Your use of memes.

Understanding memes.

And, of course, anything posted online.

The problem is as soon as you accept one of society's tools to distinguish yourself, you no longer distinguish yourself. When status symbols were rare, they had social and economic value. We keep chasing the satisfaction of status symbols not realizing they're a devalued currency. The more accessible something is, the less value it possesses.

## Inflation Is on the Rise

As a communicator and coach, currency comes in a couple of forms. Publishing a book deal and having an email list. A book says someone was willing to invest money in promoting your idea, and that you dared to write it. An email list means someone decided to give you their personal information so you can contact them. Both of these things have relevance to the impact of my message. But the other standard is social media following. The number of people following you implies your significance. I'd love to have a larger platform to share with online. But I'll never forget my short-lived business manager in 2013. Upon hearing me ask him to come up with a strategy to grow our follower base and engagement, he announced that he'd solved it the next day. He'd gone online that night and bought me a couple of thousand fake Instagram followers! Instead of working out a process of refining our message, delivering it with consistency and humility, his plan was to fake interest in my work, so that it would trick others into thinking they were missing out, and they'd follow me too. We should deceive people to help them escape the lies the world is selling them. Why didn't I think of that sooner?

Symbols change. They don't mean what you think they mean, and they don't have the power we give them. One way of not developing the imposter syndrome I talked about earlier is to not be an imposter. There's nothing wrong with sharing your life with others. My social media followers matter to me because they help me feel like I'm not alone on this ride. But I work to remind myself to post and share to help others change how they see the world, not change how they see me. Life's hard enough without the stress of worrying that the world will discover I'm not the status I wave around.

I've laid out the values of *identity*, *permission*, *courage*, and *generosity* in the metaphor of a compass, but can you see how they're not opposites? We hunt for the fake symbols of courage because we have a lack of permission. And seeking out permission and endorsement from the masses leads us to follow their vision. But the biggest risk of investing in creating status instead of courage is what it does to your identity.

## Courage, Not Comparison

All of life is navigation. And like the definition says, in order to navigate, you have to start with ascertaining accurately where you are. The trap of modern status symbols is that they demand you navigate your life in comparison to them. Every move up or down the ladder is determined by measuring the distance between you and others. But the only distance you should measure is the gap between your choices and your identity. People get so focused on what the world is doing, and if the world is paying attention to their lives that they forget to live their lives.

One of my old roommates used to complain that our younger roommate was terrible to golf with. I asked why, wondering if he was a bad golfer and slowed them down. No, he was a fine golfer. Dave's complaint was that "he spends more time Instagramming his shots than taking them." He couldn't seem to do anything without making sure someone else saw it. We eventually forced him to stop posting stories while riding his motorcycle. One time, he even asked me if when my name showed up as viewing his Insta-story, if I was watching or just swiping past. He's a great guy. Love him, but he's from a culture that believes if a tree falls in the woods, and no one is around to hear it, it's because the tree didn't have an Instagram account.

You want to go somewhere. You want to live beyond your circumstance. The only way is an old way. You have to distinguish yourself with distinguishing action. You have to be willing to do things that others are afraid of. Decisions and actions are the only ways you can go from where you are to the person you want to be. You can stand out because the world recognizes your status or you can stand out because the world sees your deeds. One will survive you, the other dissolves like a viral video.

Don't worry about everyone else. Let them look on. Let them learn. And on occasion enjoy their applause. But don't confuse their perception of your character for the reality. The courage required to live in the direction of you will never be confused with the new symbols the world sells. You're going to have to do the work, build up your strength, and learn to recognize the truth. It's going to be hard. You'll question if it's worth it. But in the end, the impact on your life and your world is sweeter than any dessert. And no amount of pedometer tapping could justify it.

14

# THE FORMULA

Find a purpose to serve, not a lifestyle to live.
—*Criss Jami*

A s a child, I loved our house around holidays. Mom would tell us to "go get the decorations." Christmas was an event, with multiple boxes and bags that would be the talk of the town, but the other holidays were cardboard things we'd gotten at the drugstore over the years. Paper hearts for the windows for Valentine's Day. A cornucopia taped to the dishwasher for Thanksgiving.

Halloween was interesting. The amount of decorations we put up was often dependent upon how much scorn you might receive from whatever local pastor had decided that Halloween was evil that particular year. At the least, we had pumpkins, but my mom never liked things that skewed dark or mystical. So, looking back, it's odd that she indulged my brother Greg and let him buy a cardboard Dracula face with fangs from Merrow's department store with his allowance.

My childhood home was a hundred-year-old house in Maine that was in a perpetual state of renovation for many years. It had a steep curving staircase that went up the middle to the bedrooms. It never had a working light in the hall, which meant that by memory you had to dodge the nails that worked themselves out of the floorboards. I lost many socks to those old, uneven floors as I schlepped to the bathroom each night.

The bathroom run was something I did a lot. I was a bed-wetter much longer than you'd like to think I was, and my mother's mantra was "always be sure to get up and go." I was happy to oblige when I would wake up. In fact, my track record was improving until one night.

Half-eyed, I dragged my seven-year-old self out of bed and stumbled through the door. My zombie walk into the hall was interrupted when I discovered not only had Greg bought the Dracula face, he'd taped it to the wall between our bedroom and the bathroom after I went to sleep. If it's possible to be petrified and dancing at the same time, that night, I was. With nothing but the streetlights and shadows to guide me, I sized up my options. It was clear: Peeing the bed was always preferred to getting eaten by a vampire.

The next morning, as I hauled my wet sheets to the laundry room, my mom demanded the vampire's removal. I'll never forget my brother's protest, aimed not toward my mom but at me: "It's just cardboard. What's the big deal?"

He was right, of course. It was just cardboard, but to my mind, the truth was it was cardboard that wanted to suck my blood.

Poor Greg. My lack of courage spelled the end to a moment of independence and a waste of his allowance. But no amount of telling me not to be scared would have gotten me to the bathroom that week. Logic, intimidation, encouragement—none of it mattered. Real courage isn't just a matter of choice; it's also a matter of truth. There's a formula for it.

## Break It Down

I've been captivated by the concept of courage most of my professional life. Our priorities reveal our hopes. Afraid as a child, I want to be courageous as an adult. I've read and interviewed people all over the world trying to understand what courage is, what it isn't, and how it grows. I would watch war movies with my dad and try to imagine how soldiers could do such difficult things. I'd ask how they could do it, but the answer I got was that they just did. If courage was based on some special reserve that people had, I was in trouble. But I noticed there was a formula and broke it into factors.

I first focused in on the action. Having the Clifton Strength of Activator, the action gets my attention. Action is courageous; lack of action is not. But it doesn't work in reverse. Sometimes, the most courageous thing to do is nothing. You don't respond to someone lashing out in pain. You don't leave when it's hard. You stand in stillness, listening instead of medicating discomfort with momentum. My definition didn't work.

I thought about the danger. Was danger the key to courage? Could dangerous action be the element that transformed our lives? Had society insulated us from harm to the point that we were no longer courageous because we didn't have to be? By this logic, the only courageous people left would be those risking life and limb. Danger wasn't the thing. In the end, it wasn't one thing; it was multiple. We need to understand how they all come together to live courageous lives.

## More Than the Sum of Its Parts

### Action

Courage isn't one thing; it's the result of mixing the right things. It's the combination of elements that produce a reaction and result.

The first element is the most obvious: action. You can't be courageous if you don't act. Knowledge without action is useless. I had a government client I was advising. He was convinced of his stellar and brave reputation because he'd never taken a bribe, and there were no public scandals during his tenure. He may have never received a bribe, but the reason he was scandal-free was that he refused to investigate. He knew his staff was claiming travel per diem for trips they never took, but he refused to look into it. His reputation would be contaminated by what an inquiry would find. Not seeing is one thing; willful blindness is another. But knowledge isn't the only thing useless without action. Opinion is too.

This one frustrates me. We have polarized politics, hysterical media, and people up in arms with complaints about everything. There's no shortage of offered judgments. Everyone wants to critique, but few want to contribute. Hashtag activism is in no way active. The majority of the Nigerian schoolgirls still didn't come home. And more are kidnapped each year. Honorable candidates for office can't be found, and if they are, people won't go the polls to elect them. And I've sat in rooms where people decry the corporate prison system and the number of people incarcerated but only take action if it is to block the opening of a transitional house in their neighborhood.

A 2017 MSNBC poll reported that almost two-thirds of US millennials (63%) think the US is on the wrong track. But almost the same number (59%) are optimistic about their own future. Huh? Unless you're all moving out of the country, where do you think this alternate positive reality is going to exist? You can't have one without the other. You can believe your country is on the wrong track, but you can't think you're removed from the consequences and obligations.

A truth that doesn't lead to action isn't truth. We live out our truth in our choices. A wise person once said, "What you say is irrelevant; what you do is what you believe." Information isn't courageous, but the information we act on can be. Action in our courageous formula is action taken to confront, overcome, or remove fear. Action for action's sake is never courageous, but action taken in response to fear can be.

If the first element of courage is action, the second element is fear.

## Fear

Fear is an emotion. It's a biological reaction to a believed potential danger, pain, or harm. It's chemical and involuntary. If you can't have courage without fear, and you can't have fear without risk, pain, or harm, then courage and potential suffering are inseparable. If there is no chance that the moment you're in could go wrong, it's not courageous. You may be excited, but you're not courageous. This is what can make courage challenging to find in everyday life. We don't like pain, we avoid danger, and we shun anyone who could bring us harm.

I've begun consulting on a security project in Nigeria. Asked by a friend to describe my reentry into western life after three weeks abroad, I told him it's like being dipped in Novocain. My security and justice consulting work is always in fragile environments that confront you twenty-four hours a day. Avoiding suicide bombers, remembering to hug and kiss the men but never shake hands with the women, planning for intermittent power outages and unique smells, closing your mouth in the shower, and never, ever rinsing your toothbrush in the sink, you are always aware of your environment.

The first moments back in more developed cities, you begin to feel the drip of medication as the concerns of the former world dissolve into oblivion one by one. The air is clean, the airline lounges are stocked, and I always stand motionless in the airport bathroom watching the water pass over my hands down the drain, not believing it's drinkable. Consumption-based societies exist to meet every demand and alleviate every discomfort, and this is why courage in the developed world gets more difficult to find.

The direction of *you* is a course that will bring you into proximity with pain. It has to. Where you are and where the world wants you to stay is comfortable. But you need to see pain and the resulting fear as harbingers of a season of courage. Danger shouldn't be avoided. It should be welcomed. But there's a critical word in the definition of fear. Fear is an emotion based on a belief of potential danger, pain, or harm. Fear is based on what you believe. Therefore, an element of courage is truth.

## Truth

Truth is the yeast in the bread of courage. Without it, the necessary transformation of all other elements can't occur. As a single guy, I've never made homemade bread outside of a bread machine, but I grew up with a mom who made it every Saturday for us. I've got the basics down. Flour, sugar, salt, yeast, and water are mixed and combined. The water interacts with the protein in flour to create a gooey substance, and when kneaded together, it becomes elastic like a balloon. But you need something to fill the air pockets. Yeast is alive. It's a fungus. It eats sugar. As it does, it produces carbon dioxide, much like we do. The released gas and alcohol infiltrates the dough through tiny pockets, letting it rise and expand. Then it's baked. The taste, texture, and appearance that we love about bread are dependent on the quality of the yeast. Yeast is critical to bread as truth is to courage. But much like yeast in bread, we never notice the importance of truth until it's missing.

The ingredients in the recipe, like the elements in our formula for courage, all exist independently, but they need a catalyst to transform each into something different from what it was before. As yeast alters the flour and sugar, truth changes our perception of fear and our choice of action. The greatest focus in developing courage is in developing your grasp on truth.

I was watching the movie *Prometheus* on a plane. It was the scene where the android David, longing to be more human, is mimicking Peter O'Toole in *Lawrence of Arabia*. Yeah, derivative, I know.

It's the famous moment after Lawrence has extinguished a lit match by squeezing it out without flinching. William Potter attempts it himself and cries out that it hurts and demands to know, "What is the trick?" To which, Lawrence utters the famous words: "Of course it hurts. The trick, William Potter, is not minding that it hurts."

I'm afraid this captures the modern concept of courage. This is how we used to tell people to be courageous. Just ignore pain. Don't admit you're afraid. If you're worthy, you'll learn not to mind that it hurts. Good soldiers suck it up and tune out the noise. The strong force themselves to go on. We think we can "bootstrap" our way to courage. We understand that fear is an element of courage, but we think the key is denial and action. That leaves too many of us with limited options for developing courage.

The most common is to deny all fear, but this doesn't work. Or if it does work, it's only temporary. Soldiers who never blinked in battle but flinch at plastic bags on the road driving to the grocery store have learned that fear can only be denied so long. It's called *post*-traumatic stress for a reason.

That leaves us with the option of "not minding that it hurts." Just do it. Push yourself on. Don't stop. Again, this will work until it doesn't. Overcoming fear because you're conditioned to, not because you believe you're strong enough, is not sustainable.

For fear and action to become courage, you need to add truth.

Truth is incredible. It works on everything. Truth softens our fears and strengthens our resolve. It takes momentary success and turns it into a tool of resilience. For this reason, in developing courage in ourselves and others, we need to spend more time focusing on truth and less on pain avoidance and rote action. And identity and permission are the truths that change.

## Sacrifice

I lived in Coronado, California, for six years. It's a small town on an island in San Diego Bay, and it's also the home to the North Island Naval Air Station and the Amphibious Assault Base (also known as Pacific—Navy SEAL Command). There were lots of team guys (Seals) in my life. One afternoon during our regular lunch at Coronado Brewing Company, I laid out for my buddy Doug my theory of danger, truth, action, and courage, thinking he'd be right on board. He wasn't. "That doesn't work," he said. Risk can't determine if an act is courageous. He and his brothers had HALO jumped (High Altitude, Low Opening) from airplanes hundreds of times to avoid detection while working to capture enemies and rescue friends. There was danger, and it was courageous. But it wasn't the act of physical risk that makes it courageous. He said he knew skydivers that were just adrenaline junkies. I hadn't thought of that. We confuse adventure and adrenaline for courage.

I've hiked the "O" circuit twice and the "W" in Chilean Patagonia five times. I've camped out in tents at 14,000 feet and crossed the Salkantay Pass in Peru on my way to Machu Picchu. I've hiked the Khumbu of Nepal. And I've cycled the coast from San Francisco to Los Angeles four times. All of those were dangerous and adventurous, but not a bit of it was courageous.

The courage demanded to move in the direction of you will not be a rush. It's not an adventure. But then what is it?

I used to teach that the formula for courage was this:

FEAR x TRUTH x ACTION = COURAGE

But I left out an element: sacrifice.

My midnight tale of bathroom woe was almost courageous. It had the potential. All the elements of the formula were there. It had fear: confrontation with the prince of darkness in the hallway. There was truth: I knew that murder by Dracula at midnight would be more permanent than murder by my mom in the morning.

And there was action. Unfortunately, a cold night in damp sheets did nothing to confront, remove, or overcome my fear. I was so close.

But even if I'd taken a breath, charged past the fangs, and dodged the nails in the floorboards, would making it to the bathroom have been courageous? No, because there was no sacrifice. I thought I was about to *be* a sacrifice, but I didn't *make* a sacrifice.

Surrendering something valued or desired for the sake of something with a higher claim: This is the definition of sacrifice. And it's sacrifice, holding the value of someone else's life higher than their own, that transforms a group of guys choosing to jump out of a plane from adrenaline junkies into elite protectors. This is why some of the most challenging choices still aren't courageous. The truth you believe has to be strong enough that you're willing to let go of something you want and act on a higher priority.

> *Surrendering something valued or desired for the sake of something with a higher claim: This is the definition of sacrifice.*

The courage that's needed to go from planning with permission to moving toward that goal demands that you make decisions on values higher than what's usual. Taking risky action, releasing something you held dear, or reordering your priorities—all sacrifice demands faith in something greater than yourself. People seek this greater priority in a number of ways. Work, family, causes, and faith. For me, I'm a follower of Jesus. I find that his example of love and service inject themselves into my decision-making formula when I have to decide to be courageous or not. Wherever you find your reason to sacrifice, it must be beyond the ordinary. You have to have something worth sacrificing for.

So, here's our formula for courage.

Fear x Truth x Sacrifice x Action = Courage

It wouldn't have helped me avoid an unfortunate night in damp pajamas, but it applies to the significant moments of life. The question is, will it help with the insignificant ones as well?

# 15

# COMMON COURAGE

Courage is found in unlikely places.
—J. R. R. Tolkien

I was invited to speak to executives at Bank of America in Washington, DC, some years ago. It was to be an afternoon talk on strengths-based personal development. My contact asked if I would also meet with leaders of the bank's professional affinity groups for a small dinner the night before. Always looking for business development, I agreed.

Upon arrival at the restaurant, I got hustled off to a back room where they were waiting. Dinner sessions are interesting as they're often an attempt by the client to be casual, but there's a definite expectation that I should be "on." I've since learned to eat before going to one.

We chatted over menus, ordered, and then I did my thing. Over passing plates, pouring wine, and the long table of executives, I talked about strengths and identity and the need to hold passion as a valid tool for navigating career and life. There were nods around the table. I started my party trick where strangers share with me their Clifton Strengths themes and, using their five results alone, I tell them their loves, hates, and what they fight about with their significant others. I'm not convinced it has much impact on the world, but people find it entertaining.

After "reading people's mail" for an hour, I took questions and comments. This was when I lost folks. There were the questions on talent compatibility. There were inquiries on how to get people to change to be less annoying. And there were the occasional "How do I navigate to a new position?" queries. I danced my mix of response without prescription, given the little interaction I had had with these people.

A woman in her mid-forties said, "I love your words on the importance of passion. Too bad it's too late for me. For years I dreamed of working for the Peace Corp. in refugee centers. I was passionate about it in college. If I'd understood this concept, then my life would be different."

Not restraining myself as much as I should, I spun around and said, "It's not too late!" She assured me it was. She had a job. She had a husband, kids, and a mortgage. Soon college tuition and retirement would come. It was too late.

Sometimes things hook me, and I don't let it go as I should.

I laughed and shot back, "It's not too late. You can still work for the Peace Corp. Maybe not today, maybe not tomorrow, but it is possible. The kids move out. You and your husband can downsize your mortgage. You can scrimp on vacations and save the money. You have made choices in the past that are choosing for you today, but you could change that. It takes common courage and the desire to want your life to embody your identity."

*The raw ingredients for courage are everywhere.*
*All that is needed is you.*

The room got silent. It had become all too real. And confronted with the ownership of the moment, people were over my party trick. Picking up my glass, I pulled the ripcord on my well-worn escape chute joke and laughed, "But what do I know?"

## All "Decisions" Great and Small

What do I know?

I know that fear is common, and people take action every day in an attempt to alleviate it. While discouraging, this truth means something significant: The raw ingredients for courage are everywhere. All that is needed is you.

Courage is more than soldiering, rescuing, and standing up to attack. The exceptional thing about it is that, if you insert a shot of sacrifice into your decision-making when you're afraid, everyday moments become courageous.

The small business owner who cuts his own salary instead of cutting heads.

The woman who ignores the demeaning voice of her incomplete list and checks on a friend.

The father who is afraid he's insignificant at work but prioritizes his child's soccer game over office hours.

The MBA who opts for community outreach over corporate consulting.

The mother who refuses to tolerate abuse because her kids need to know it's not okay.

We're going to increasing extremes to inject meaning into our lives. We're looking outward when we need to be looking within. Imagine every day as an opportunity to be courageous. But this only works if we're searching for meaning and not public acclaim. Common courage comes with no reward. The cost of your sacrifice is a price others never see. The practice of common courage is the antidote to a meaningless life, and it is a litmus test of where we find meaning.

We're back to identity and permission. It's easy to overplay the compass metaphor, and I lay out the individual pieces to help people understand each element, but they all connect. Common courage demands that even the simple decisions have a slice of sacrifice. But as we know, sacrifice is releasing something valued or desired for the sake of something believed to be of higher value. If you don't have a vision that is bigger than the moment you're in, there is nothing more significant than the immediate. Speed, autonomy, clarity—in the absence of vision, these are of the highest value. But why don't we have insight that cuts through the noise? Because we haven't internalized our identity and the capacity of our talent and passion.

This is the place where a disconnected life begins to show its cracks. You can be ignorant of your talents and how they connect to your passion, and no one will know. You can spin words of vision and posture permission, but the nature of vision ensures few will hold you accountable. Courage, especially common courage, is only present if the essentials are connected. It's evident in decisions great and small. The courageous life demands an identity and the vision of permission and sacrifice in decision-making. But in time, another factor comes into play: Our choices that choose.

## Choices That Choose

Near the end of most of my Clifton Strengths workshops, someone asks what my themes are. The subtext is the desire to compare my profile to theirs. There are one or two every session that will come tell me they would love to do what I do. For many years, I've said they can. It's a long road, but it's open to anyone. Get Clifton Strengths certified, find your unique application for the tool, and then share your gift with anyone who will let you. I've stopped counting the number of sessions I did for small groups in living rooms and nonprofits that couldn't afford it. I didn't care. Any engagement was a chance to refine my skills and build another relationship.

It's meaningful when younger clients want to follow this path. People love helping other people, and they like the thought of impacting the world in the way they're experiencing it. Being asked for ways to do what I do is the highest compliment I can receive. After all these years, I've refined my answer to the question, "How can I do what you do?" Unlike the early years, my response now is "Start saving money." This catches most off guard. They look at me perplexed. They want the courses to take and the people to talk to. What could savings have to do with being a consultant? You can't afford to build a business if you can't afford to do it cheaply. I suggest they downsize. They might want to put off having kids or getting a mortgage. Baffled is how I'd describe their looks.

> *Every day we make choices that*
> *will choose for us later.*

I'm not saying coaches can't have children and homes. I know many who have both. But to make the shift from employee to an independent consultant is to embrace uncertainty. Uneven months of income, unexpected expenses, and finding the balance between investment and sucker is difficult. It can be impossible if you have previous demands and debt. I explain this to anyone who will ask, but it doesn't seem to sink in. This isn't about money, and I'm not trying to disqualify anyone, but there's a simple truth that is too often overlooked. Every day we make choices that will choose for us later.

- Children now vs. children later
- Renting vs. buying
- New car vs. used car

- Old phone vs. new phone
- Vacation vs. staycation

Not one of these choices is better than the other, but each impacts future decisions. Decisions move us toward or away from our identity. Some are major, and some are minor, but each multiplies our options or limits them. This has been a hard-learned lesson for me. I've made significant decisions about not being in a relationship and not having kids of my own to be able to be more connected to other people and their situations. It wasn't an easy decision, but it's a clear one. I have a greater challenge with smaller choices. I justify buying a new phone since it takes better photos, and social media is essential to my brand. Despite the fact no one complains about my current phone, and money decreasing my company debt would have a greater impact on people. I make the decisions in the present and forget the pain of the future.

This is our problem. We disconnect the choices of today from the impact of tomorrow. It's not difficult to want to include sacrifice in our decision-making when the cause we serve is imminent. We pull off the highway to help save lives and property when we come upon an accident, but we won't tolerate slowpokes or be patient enough to prevent accidents in the future. We live like slaves to the immediate. I once heard a professor of theology say that one of the profound realities of God's is that when it comes to time, he exists outside of it, but humans cannot escape it. This feels true. Immediate gratification, efficient decision-making, deserving today versus receiving tomorrow—these daily choices will choose for us later. A single choice may not have an impact, but a chorus of them will shout over the voice of any vision that doesn't give way.

## Mo' Money

Choices that choose is a rule that impacts most decisions in life but is the most pronounced with time and money. A truth that was shared with me years ago but still makes me insecure is this: If you want to know what a person cares about, look at their checkbook and their calendar. Who are you spending time with, and what are you spending money on? People will tell me they want to get out of their ruts and they want lives that matter. But they are still giving time to friends who shut them down or mock them. They're letting insignificant affirmations hook them instead of investing in a future result. And they're allowing the cultural voice of entitlement to drown out the truth of earning the right to experience an extraordinary life. This realization can be disheartening, but there is hope. It works the other way too.

Choices today that choose for us tomorrow is a truth that can give us hope. For everything that we've done in the past to limit options today, today's decisions can move you closer to freedom tomorrow. You're never locked in. You are not too far gone. You can cancel your cable and use the money to pay off debt. Go through your closet and open that eBay/craigslist account. Throw a modern-day yard sale. Make a "do not buy" list for every other month and start watching your savings. Prioritize relationships that will return to you as much as you give them. They may not be relationships of equals, but there are multiple ways to feel the return of that effort.

Common courage is the sacrificing decision despite fear and a personal need. You can build this into your life. In Gallup's book *Wellbeing*, they reference the impact of defaults in daily life. The default is something that was chosen once and left unchanged. It's like the time you bought movie tickets online, and just before checkout, you failed to notice the checkbox that signed you up for junk mail for eternity. While many boxes are blank and require you to check the box to signup, statistics show that while we may not check a box to register, we are less likely to uncheck the box. This checked box is called a default opt-in. You didn't "opt-in" to anything; the page default was opting you in. This can work in our favor.

Gallup found that exercise scheduled before noon is more likely to be done than exercise planned after work. And savings pulled out of an account on the first of the month is more likely to be saved than money scheduled for the last of the month. Frameworks we build once can decide for us over and over. Remarkable power results when common courage meets choices that choose. You can pre-schedule date nights and family time. You can budget for courses and certificates that will get you out of a hated job. You can save for your second career with the same passion you save for your child's tuition. It's simple steps in the direction of you. It's like the Heath brothers said in their book *Switch*: We need to practice asymmetrical decision-making. Our solutions for life must be smaller than our problem. If the solutions are as complex as the problems, they never get implemented. Seek common courage and recognize choices that choose, and your life will change.

## Practice, Practice, Practice

Knowing the courageous choice and making it in the moment are two very different things. In *The Power of Habit,* Charles Duhigg talks about how our resolve can be true but our self-control evaporates in the face of stress and the unexpected. The answer is to plan to be courageous. This works on multiple fronts.

Orthopedic patients who were being sent home from the hospital and needed to keep moving had to create plans to deal with the unexpected to get their steps in.

My friend Angelo Poli is the founder of MetPro and a nutrition and fitness consultant to the biggest names in professional sports and entertainment. One of his keys to success with clients is pre-planning how to eat healthy when you're somewhere unexpected. You have to have snacks, and you have to have a strategy.

It's not a lack of conviction that derails us; it's a lack of planning for the unknown.

If you are going to prioritize your family, you need to practice your responses before your boss asks you to stay late.

Rehearse in your head holding on to the truth when you're feeling afraid.

Pre-play in your mind a vision of yourself keeping your cool and honoring your values.

We need to plan to be courageous. We need to understand who we are, where we're going, and what it will take to get there. That's identity, permission, and courage. But we need to plan for the unforeseen. We need to think about what might happen. How will we deal with confrontation? What can support us when fatigue overwhelms our resolve? Simple plans, default options, and choices that choose are effective tools for moving in the direction of you. If we understand them, practice using them, and then keep them a priority, our day-to-day lives can become stories of common courage, I promise. But then again, as I told the people in the restaurant that night, what do I know?

Part 4

# GENEROSITY:
# How Do We Keep
# from Getting Lost?

# 16

# DEFINING GENEROSITY

> Attention is the rarest and purest form of generosity.
> —*Simone Weil*

M y buddy Jeremy is a rare friend. He's a great guy who supports and encourages me but also understands me. What he does for the Gallup Organization internally, I do externally. We often commiserate on the challenges of trying to transform clients' thinking as we travel the world. It doesn't happen often, but we try to connect whenever we can.

Some years ago, I got a last-minute message that Jeremy was flying into Orange County and asking if I could meet him for dinner. By some miracle, I was home and available and ran up to Newport.

When I picked him up at the curb, he was on the phone. That wasn't unusual for him, but then he wouldn't get off. Patient at first, I started getting annoyed as I drove and he continued. At last, he paused and said, "Sorry, Mike, but I've got to take this."

It turns out that Jeremy's last-minute trip had caused him to miss his son's first day of junior high. Jeremy and his wife Jill are exceptional parents and never miss milestones. And until this night, Jeremy had never missed Joseph's first day of school before.

Turning down the radio, I started focusing in on his conversation. "Hey, buddy, you okay? ... Yeah, I'm sorry I'm missing tomorrow."

From the tone of Jeremy's voice, I could tell his son was nervous. My heart went out to Joseph. I knew that feeling. To this day, I'll work in a war zone before signing up to redo junior high school.

After a little listening, there was a pause, and Jeremy asked, "Are you afraid?" I could hear Joseph say, "Yes."

Jeremy responded, "Well, it's okay to be afraid, buddy."

And then Jeremy asked his twelve-year-old son a question I'll never forget.

"But what do we do when we're scared?"

What do we do when we're scared? What do you mean? When we're scared, we stop, we cry, we eat ice cream, workout, binge-watch TV. What was he asking? Besides, what kind of question was that? Focused on their exchange, I saw Jeremy nod and say:

"That's right, Joe. When we're afraid, we focus on someone else."

Jeremy kept going, "There are probably other kids who are afraid. What if you could be their friend? When we focus on others, we feel less afraid for ourselves."

This is the paradox and power of generosity. It is a focus on others, but it's a gift to ourselves.

## The Source of Our Courage

The final point on our compass is generosity. It follows courage because it's the value that transforms our choices. The formula for courage is Fear x Truth x Sacrifice x Action = Courage. If the world provides the fear, and identity and permission provide the truth, then generosity can give us something worth sacrificing for. Generosity is not about giving others money; it's about giving part of our story to become a part of theirs.

The traditional definition of generosity is what you'd expect: readiness or willingness in giving. But when I looked it up in the dictionary, it's the second definition that challenged me most. That definition said, "Generosity is freedom from meanness or smallness of mind or character." Freedom from the smallness of mind. I like the thought that a lack of generosity is slavery to a small mind. Generosity is having a view of the world bigger than ourselves. Therefore, cultivation of generosity comes in nurturing a broader view of the people around us. It reveals itself in our thoughts, feelings, and behaviors.

Our generosity reveals itself in how we see others. One of the greatest things you can give someone is the gift of being seen. But this seeing is about more than behavior. Do you recognize their humanity, potential, and their resilience through their struggle? An organization I've recently become aware of has turned this generosity of seeing into the heart of what they do. The F5 Project was started by Adam Martin, a five-time felon turned entrepreneur. Adam knows all too well the struggle of trying to rebuild a life under the shame of a conviction. Through communication, housing, employment, and more, his team is helping remove the stigma of prison and letting people be seen as more than their worst moments. What if your worst moments were documented for public review and you could never change it? Would there be any gift as sweet as being seen for more than just that mistake? Generosity can be expressed in the way we think about others.

Generosity is also found in our feelings about the people around us. Do you let yourself emotionally engage with the people in your life? This was hard for me for a long time. I wondered if friends were less committed to relationships than I was. I hated feeling needy. If I cared more than they cared, it would say something about my value. It was all about me. The rejection was too big of a risk. I developed this belief that relationships only worked in a zero-sum world. If I gave more than I received from someone, I was a sucker and would end up on the losing end forever. My mindset was one of scarcity. There was a limited amount of emotional energy, and I should only offer it to the worthy, or I'd end up the loser. As I began the journey I describe at the beginning of this book, my source of value and affirmation was in everyone else's hands. This was a risky way to live. As I understood my identity, I learned that my emotional capacity is based on my talents. It's hardwired in me and is a renewable resource. It's never lost unless it's not given away.

Feelings are meant to be expressed. To practice generosity, start texting people when they come to mind. "Thought of you today. Wanted you to know you matter." Do that a few times a week, or anytime someone comes to mind. You'll be amazed at how encouraging that is to others and how it makes you feel. You will realize that even as you give support to others, generosity gives back to you.

The last area of practice for generosity is in our behavior. Acts of service, words of kindness, and the simplicity of making eye contact can free us from the slavery of small-mindedness. Joseph's decision to befriend others who were scared opened his mind to reconsider his own fear. This is the power of generosity to change the narrative in our heads and expand our thinking.

## Keeping on Track

These practices of generosity allow our lives to intersect with others. Much like the grove of redwoods I talked about, as our paths intertwine, we depend on and support one another. This matters because you need to be part of a story bigger than yourself if you're going to stay on track moving in the direction of you. Personal motivation wanes when things get hard. No amount of discipline and commitment can overcome every obstacle. We need a cause or story beyond ourselves to connect to. It's like gravity: It can draw us on. Like Frankl said, it's the universe that's going to be asking questions that only you can answer. The significant story doesn't need just anything—it needs you. Generosity isn't just being selfless; it's the act of sharing your best self.

> *Personal motivation wanes*
> *when things get hard.*

One of my favorite books of 2017 was Angela Duckworth's *Grit*. Former McKinsey consultant and Macarthur Genius Grant recipient, she researches why some of the toughest people quit things they really want. Her initial focus was West Point Cadets. She has since expanded her research and now speaks all over the world. One of her findings explained the power of generosity and its connection to identity and permission. She found that the most resilient or grittiest, people were those with intrinsic motivation. This motivation was based on the satisfaction achieved from reaching goals. But the fascinating part is that the goals had to feel like they were for the greater good. The most transactional of workers possessed the ability to be motivated if they felt like what they were doing was a calling. Waiters, school teachers, executives, and sanitation workers—the more their job felt like it was a calling, the higher the achievement. But for it to feel like a calling, they had to have a natural interest in it. Sounds a lot like understanding talent.

Understanding your talents and finding people to share them with will begin to give you something worth sacrificing for. And this higher calling will keep you on the road when your own motivation has gone. Think about others, express your feelings, and if you're as smart as my friend Joseph, you'll offer your support to those as scared as you.

# 17

# MULTIPLICATION

Individually, we are one drop.
Together, we are an ocean.
—*Ryunosuke Satoro*

Some years ago, my friend Dwight Powery began doing something that sounded insane. He joined a charity bike ride called the California Coast Classic. A charity ride isn't unusual, but the fact that it's 550 miles down the coast of California is. He'd never been a cyclist, but in short order, he had purchased a bike, poured himself into some spandex, and was hitting the road every weekend to train. He was a man on a mission, and that mission was to have an impact in memory of his daughter Christiana.

A few years before, Christiana had suddenly passed away from complications from a rare autoimmune disease called dermatomyositis. What should have been a treatable chronic condition took an unexpected turn, and after barely ninety days of hospitalization, she left us. A few years later, some of her doctors at Stanford Children' Hospital told Dwight they heard that the Arthritis Foundation had a ride called the California Coast Classic. Christiana had juvenile arthritis, and it's in the same family of diseases as dermatomyositis. They decided they were riding in her honor and wanted to know if he wanted to join them. There's a power that comes when grieving turns into action.

Dwight did it alone with the doctors his first year, but it wasn't long until his oldest daughter Evelyn was riding. His wife Maria joined the next year, and then Serena made it a family affair. Before long, they were a recruiting machine for Team "Also Touch."

*There's a power that comes when grieving turns into action.*

The team name came from the final line in Christiana's journal. Each day in the hospital, she'd write her thoughts and feelings, ending each entry with a prayer that "Jesus touch..." and she'd list out the kids on her floor. The last words she ever wrote were "And Jesus, please also touch ..." She never finished the sentence, leaving the words "also touch" her final gift. The ride became a platform to tell the story of their brave girl whose struggle and courage provided medical breakthroughs and possibilities for others. I couldn't resist their passion for very long.

I've now done the ride four times, and if you're looking for an experience you'll never forget for a cause you've never heard about, you should check it out. But beyond the views, the comradery, the fantastic food, and the support of the Arthritis Foundation, my experience on the final day of my first year was transformational for me.

After seven days on the road, we were making the final push from Ventura Beach to the Yahoo Center in L.A. Having experienced it multiple times now, I've learned that the last day is the best of times and the worst of times. By day eight, adaptation to extreme mileage has set in, the finish line feels close, but there's a stretch of rolling hills that reminds you that nothing comes easy. Cresting the last large grade, I coasted to the stoplight in front of the sprawling lawn of Pepperdine University on the Pacific Coast Highway in Malibu.

Focused on just getting it done, the team had gotten spread out in the final hours, and waiting at the light, for the first time in days, I was alone. It felt good. I took a breath and, looking at my daily route guide, realized the biggest climbing challenge of the week was behind me. I was within hours of completing something that seemed impossible a week ago.

I felt stirred and strong, and just before I got too proud of my 250 pounds propped in spandex waiting for a green light, the Plan B cycling team pulled up next to me. I'm pretty sure these guys were world-class cyclists. If they weren't, they at least looked the part: slick, skinny and liquid in their all-black riding gear. I was in awe. Seeing the logo on my jersey, they asked about the tour. Forgetting all the pain and struggle, I sold the views, weather, and how I'd do it all again. And that was something I hadn't once thought before that moment. As the light turned green, they said goodbye and pulled off the line in unison, leaving me wobbling behind.

To see expert cycling up close is something to behold. When watching it on TV, the mass of competing riders is called a peloton. But teams within the peloton actually ride on what they call a line because that's what it is. It doesn't seem like anything special, but riding on a line is magical and must be well managed.

Team line is a configuration that adjusts and changes collectively. The smooth motion of cyclists through space creates pockets of air that are backfilled and, like the wing of a plane, pull riders along. It's called drafting. This formation allows riders to go faster and expend less energy. But there must be someone at the front to create the draft. This rider is generating all the thrust that pulls the group along but receives none of the benefits. For this reason, the lead of the line is a rotating responsibility. As speed increases and the powerful legs of the leader tire, the head of the line peels off and coasts to the back so the rider behind can take their place. It's impressive to watch.

As the team line formed as they pulled away, a rush of adrenaline got the best of me. Forgetting my place, caliber of cycling, and the eight days of lactic acid in my legs, I jumped on their line.

Now drafting isn't just a vacation behind other riders. To be on the line, you have to keep up with the line. I began spinning my pedals as fast as I could. It was all I could do to reach them and stay behind the last rider. But as I approached him, the magic kicked in. The closer I got, the faster I went, and by the time there were less than six inches between tires, I felt like I had a motor on my bike.

Flying through Malibu that Saturday morning, we broke twenty-four miles per hour … then twenty-six … then twenty-eight. I can't remember our max speed, but our line was a blur, and I was its tail. It felt like flying! The higher the speed, the more it felt like we were in slow motion. It was like being in the middle of something I'd never experienced before—true unity. But suddenly I was afraid.

A signal passed through the line, and the leader peeled off and made his way toward the back. Convinced that my tagalong time was over, I prepared to make room for him to drop me from the group. But as he approached, instead of cutting me off from the crew, he dropped back behind me!

One by one they peeled off and took positions behind me. With each rider, I got closer to the front. I didn't know what I was going to do. In fact, it was all I could do to keep up.

I didn't belong here. I was a poser, a fraud. Even being pulled by the draft, it was taking all I had to keep my legs going. There would be no way I could lead. As I started to motion that I was going to bail off the line, the guy behind the guy behind me shouted, "C'mon, man! You can do this. Stick it!" So I did. I rode like the wind. Cheesy, I know, but even writing this brings a smile to my face. I held my ground and kept on spinning. Not only did they include me, but they also protected me. One by one, they bypassed me to take the lead. Each one pulling me along, providing what I couldn't: the pace, protection, and momentum I could never achieve by myself.

My final miles to the finish were melting away as we rounded the point near Pacific Palisades. Flying past a resting group of my fellow riders, my buddy Danny said I was a green flash (my jersey) in a mob of black, and no one could believe it.

That morning, in a group of strangers, I did things that I could never do on my own. I went farther than I had ever gone. And I went faster than I would ever go. This is the power of generosity.

## More Together

Multiplication is the human holy grail. We thirst to be more, and anything that can extend our thoughts, efforts, and lives is pursued. This isn't just for leaders and business people. The world of technology is built on the promise of multiplying our strengths. Cook faster, clean better, share more, build stronger—we are driven by the desire to do the thing we're called to do. But life is short, and so we seek tools to have an impact beyond our years. Each innovation for the menial is meant to free up time for the substantial. But it doesn't often work that way. For each insignificant thing banished by the power of automation, a new one springs up. There's nothing wrong with seeking leverage and technology, but we need to recognize the reality of its limits. And if tech and innovation aren't the answers to living a multiplied life, then what is?

A few years ago, I got a severe cold and lost my voice. For a professional speaker, that's not a good thing. I get raspy and hoarse on occasion, but this was different. I was out of business for a few weeks before I beat the bug. My voice improved, but not much. It would last a day then be gone. Conference calls were a killer, and I had to stop having dinner meetings because I couldn't project over the din of the restaurant. After two months, my doctor referred me to an ear, nose, and throat specialist who performed the obligatory scope up the nose and down into the larynx.

I made all the oohs and ahhhs for him as he grunted back hmms and huhs. I expected a resilient infection diagnosis with a prescription for steroids and some high-dose antibiotics. It was unnerving when he sat, squared up in front of me, and said, "Looks like you've got a growth on your left vocal cord. It's not on the edge where nodes or nodules would be (a common speaker/ singer ailment). It's on the cord itself. It might be nothing. Let's give it thirty days and see if it goes away." I acted calm, but I was rattled. I booked my follow-up for the day after my return from that year's Dauphinee Adventure to Patagonia with six clients. I wanted to clear up any questions as soon as possible.

The Patagonia trip with Roberto Carlos that I wrote about in the permission section (Part 2) went so well that I've started doing them each year with clients. They usually run like clockwork, but that year, one of my team had a pre-existing condition that showed up the second day, required an emergency evacuation from the national park, and a racing five-hour ambulance run to avoid death in the middle of the night. And it's actually even more dramatic than it sounds. And after getting him settled in a hospital, I had to run back into the mountains to catch up with my crew to finish the trek. By the time we returned to the states, I was drained. I had also forgotten my scope was the next day.

Arriving at the ENT office, I was so groggy I don't remember much, but I do remember him looking at me as he finished the exam and saying, "The growth didn't shrink, and it's now changing color. We need to excise this from your cord and biopsy it to rule out cancer. The surgery isn't simple as I'll be fileting it off the flat of the cord. You could lose the use of that cord. But I expect that it will all go fine. You just need to know. Let's get a surgery date on the calendar. By the way, you won't be able to make a sound for twelve days and won't be able to project for four to five weeks. Assuming all goes well." In the immortal words of my young friend Emma, "Wait, what?"

I can't convey how little capacity I had to cope with this news. When I met my friend Danny for lunch at Estancia Resort in La Jolla, I was a zombie. Recovering from hiking, jet lag, near-death stress of a friend, potential cancer, and loss of my source of livelihood was more than I could manage. For the next weeks, the questions swirled. I couldn't have the surgery right away since I had pre-booked clients that I couldn't push out past my recovery dates. And if I lost my voice for a more extended period, I'd need the money.

I have the Clifton Strength of Command, so struggle brings out the best in me, but I wrestle on the inside. Recovery, pain, money, alone—I'd run through all the scenarios in my head, and at some point, the more significant questions found their way to the front. What if I lost my voice? What if I couldn't speak? My childhood tormentors would finally get their way. Funny to think that the reality I tried to achieve for years was now the thing I feared most.

It took time, but I began to find my center. I wouldn't give in to fear. No matter what happened, I could still find a way to impact the world. My identity wouldn't go away, I would just have to find a new way to move toward it, and a few nights before surgery, I realized how. My friend Danny Kim and I were meeting up with our buddy Ed for a quiet night around his fire pit. It was a chance to relax before the intensity began. Asking for an update, I croaked out the bullet points and the risks. A coach himself,

Ed just smiled and nodded and then said, "Well, I guess if you lose your voice this week, you'll just have to speak to the world through others." Ever have people put words to things you've only felt? I knew that was the answer.

If I was silent the next week, there were others who could sing my song. I've been blessed by friends that have sustained me and invited me into their lives. Many of them opened the door, feeling they needed me, not realizing I would need them more in the end.

I needed to continue to find words of impact and courage, but others could speak them to the world. I may lose my voice, but I didn't need to lose my calling. For the first time, I understood living a life of *getting* to do something instead of *having* to. I get to speak because I'm me. I don't have to speak to be me.

But it didn't have to go this way. It could have been different. I could have been more afraid. I could have doubled my anxiety and reinforced my narcissism. I could have demanded that my voice is the one that mattered and prioritized myself. I would have traded multiplication for addition.

Generous people live in community. They don't limit themselves to seeing people; they choose to live with people. They understand that they are more together. Their voice and impact are insular and one-dimensional in the echo chamber of isolation. There is power in giving to people in moments. It's a needed injection of momentum. But there's sustained energy for the journey in lives that are lived together. In communities of faith, commitments of teams and families that reach beyond the nuclear, they have tapped into the power of giving and receiving from each other. And if one is silent, the others will pick up that song. But you've got to be in position.

As I flew through Malibu that day, I was going faster than I'd ever gone, but I was working harder than I thought I could. The momentum and motion of those guys all grinding it out in unity called me to be more and let me experience it. But as soon as I got out of sync, the power slipped away. In the right position, I felt the pull of the draft. Too far out, I bore the brunt of the wash. And with each moment in misalignment, it was easier to drift away. Generosity provides what we long for. The chance to be more. You understand who you are. You've dreamed where you want to go. You're on the road and making choices to get there. What if I told you that you can go even further? All you've got to do is take a chance, join your life to others, find your spot, and, like the voice behind me shouted that morning, "C'mon man, stick it!"

# 18

# MOMENTS

You have not lived today until you have done something
for someone who can never repay you.

*—John Bunyan*

In 2012, I began traveling alone into Afghanistan to do pro bono leadership consulting for teams and organizations that couldn't afford support. There was plenty of international funding for transactional programs but not much for leadership development. I had fallen in love with the country and its people on previous visits and decided I wanted to be part of a long-term solution. But as much as I enjoyed the work and opportunity, it was taxing, and by the end, I always welcomed my flight out of the country.

War-zone life is one of constant confrontation. Beyond the apparent life-and-limb risk from attacks and IEDs (improvised explosive devices), the air you breathe and the lack of clean water to drink means that Kabul days can have very little rest. You have your guard up to everything around you. So, as I made my way to my seat for my exodus flight to Dubai that day, I had no time for anyone. Exhausted and self-centered, I buckled in and prayed the prayers I pray when flying in a plane manufactured in 1970. My seatmate, a young Afghan guy of about nineteen, got situated beside me and gave a hesitant smile and nod. Something about him snapped me from my funk.

As a ten-minute ground delay dragged on to thirty, my seat-mate seemed to grow concerned. Almost not understandable through his accent, he asked why we had not moved. I tried to explain what the pilot had said and assured him it would be fine.

Emboldened by my willingness to speak to him, my new friend, Samir, launched into conversation. I was engrossed. At first, it was because of the concentration required to grasp his English, but his story took hold of me over time. Topics of the plane and weather gave way to unexpected depth as I began asking where he was from and why he was traveling alone. I sat rapt as his narrative unfolded.

Five years before, after the murder of his parents, he had decided to leave his little brother with neighbors to become one of the Afghan boys that walked and hitchhiked from Kabul to the UK. This early migration was before the mass exodus to Europe that has now occurred across the region. I'd seen a special report about the journey on *60 Minutes* the previous year. I asked him if it was as bad as I'd heard. He closed his eyes and nodded. I couldn't imagine the violence and violation that comes with being a child at the hands of smugglers, criminals, and people who don't want you, all while trying to get to safety.

He made it to the UK, was given temporary asylum, and lived with a foster family. While hard, he had a better life than he'd known in Kabul. That's where he'd learned the English he was excited to practice. In the end, he was denied permanent residency in the UK. But God had smiled on him, and he had been given a permanent visa to Italy. He had returned from the UK to Afghanistan for what would be his last time to find his brother and gather up the belongings he left behind. To his sorrow, both were gone.

Sitting there, helping him make sense of his immigration packet and explaining how airport transfers worked, I couldn't get over his sense of resilience and hope. He would never see his home country again. His brother, he expected, was lost to the wind as well. He still believed that somehow his friends in Italy and his ability to work hard was going to get him through. He didn't know where he was going, but he was sure it was the right direction.

Sometimes I meet people and realize that there are giants among us. They have tapped into a capacity that we leave dormant. They stand on mountains and face crashing waves and are sure of their strength. There's a verse that people liked to share when I was a child that starts with, "Since we are surrounded by such a great cloud of witnesses …" The idea is that the generations before us watch and cheer us on. Thinking of Samir at that moment, I thought of how I wanted to cheer him on. And as I picked through my moments of courage and thought of the people that surrounded and supported me, I knew what I had to do.

## Generosity isn't what we think it is.

Like Nina Lord did when I left home at eighteen and like Adrian Carver did when I graduated college and moved to California for the first time, I knew I had to give Samir all I had. As the people began to deplane in Dubai, he gathered up the plastic grocery bag he used for a carry-on and smiled, thanking me for the help and encouragement. Overwhelmed, I grabbed for the three twenties I'd stuffed in my passport and grabbed his hand before the row moved.

He felt the cash in his palm and his eyes got big. I breathed, "Allah's blessing on you, my friend." He paused, looked at me stunned, nodded, and was gone. As I walked up the jet bridge, I realized what a culturally inappropriate thing that was to do. But

I couldn't help it. I had been moved by this deep need to be a bit player in his extraordinary life story. It was for him, but it was about me.

Generosity isn't what we think it is. It isn't about rich and poor, haves and have-nots. Generosity is about acknowledging people and responding with open hands, hearts, and minds in recognition of their humanity. Generosity is an attempt to be a part of a world bigger than our own. The moments of others that we step into change the stories of our own lives.

## Moments Matter

Much like courage, when it comes to generosity, we have over-shot the mark. We confuse generosity with philanthropy and think about it regarding financial contribution or grand gestures. But similar to common courage, generosity shared in simple moments can become the texture that distinguishes our lives. Your brush with a different world will alter your perspective in ways you couldn't have planned.

The extraordinary life, the life that is different from all the rest, the life that reacts to everyday challenges in unique ways, is one that has been altered. This life's navigation has been altered by the giving and receiving of momentary generosity along the way. The compilation of the seemingly insignificant interactions expands your view. By examining your identity, your perspective on how you can apply your talent is broadened as you see a growing need. And the emotional connection with a stranger might refine your passion. Seeing a community living by different rules, an ocean away, can convey permission and magnify your vision for wherever you could go. And the courageous in spirit, who are looking for something worth sacrificing for, may discover it's passing them on the street if they are interacting with people with anticipation.

Simple flashes of kindness are not as inconsequential as they seem. Researcher John Gottman claims kindness is a significant key to relational success. A scientist at the University of Washington, he wanted to research how couples thrived or didn't survive marriage. They invited hundreds of couples to their lab, a wired condo, for weekends of observation. The couples were asked to discuss topics, do some exercises, but were also observed doing nothing more than spending time alone. In the end, they analyzed what they called the masters and disasters of marriage.

Gottman noticed and has now developed the theory of bids. All day long, people want to connect. They make emotional bids to each other in hopes of finding the briefest of connections. Your wife gets up from the couch to get a drink and asks if she can get you something. You have a few options.

You can turn toward her, "Yes, thanks, I'd love a Coke Zero."

You can turn against her, "Do you really need to ask? You should know I want a drink!"

You can turn away, "I don't care. Do what you want to."

Not surprising, couples who turned toward each other in higher frequency had higher marital satisfaction and success. But I was intrigued to find that turning against was better than turning away. I assumed that the aggression would damage the relationship. But Gottman and his team found that the confrontation at least gave grounds for the couple to engage, even if in conflict. The single greatest threat to relationships is indifference. Being oblivious to the kindness and simple moments being offered, whether by intention or neglect, hurt the offering individual and decreased the likelihood that the kindness will ever be offered again.

This isn't limited to marriage. It happens at work, in line at the café, in the people you sit beside in church. It's best if you respond kindly; it's painful if you offer conflict, but it's devastating if you ignore. Think about it. Is there anything worse than people not responding to you? Being on hold, ignored by waiters, your kids not answering when called. We are hardwired to want people to respond and engage, even in the smallest moments. Moments of kindness are the glue that holds our journey together. It's too bad that glue is rarely seen because it's applied to the seams, and no one knows it is missing until things fall apart. Are you aware of the bids around you? Are you responsive? What's your posture to the world?

## Moments That Can Change Your Life

Like I said earlier, it's the moments you never see coming that seem to change your life. The Heath brothers are right; peaks, pits and transitions are important, but you can't expect that those are the keys to your life. Significant moments and life-changing ones aren't always the same thing. The most understated interaction can redirect your life.

In 2011, I was asked to travel to Jos, Nigeria to spend a couple weeks speaking. I'd be working with an HIV hospital in town, teach across the state, and get the chance to spend a couple days out in the bush. Never one to turn down an adventure, I agreed.

There were a lot of firsts on that trip. First time in Africa. First time traveling for two weeks never seeing more than two people of my own race. First time going two weeks without power. And it was my first two-week stretch without a shower—if you don't count standing naked in a bucket pouring water over my head one night. By the way, wet wipes are a marvel and a lifesaver.

It was also the first time I ever taught with a translator. I spoke at the clinic, and the translation that morning wasn't good. I struggled, and so did my translator. My speed was probably a problem for him, so he bailed out afterwards and pushed another young guy to babysit me for the day. We connected right away, and he made a painful experience bearable since I knew he could interpret and not just translate me. It was supposed to be for one day, but the next morning, he took the week off and traveled with us to the regions four hours into the bush. By the end of my time, he had become my brother. I don't know the moment it happened, but it did.

As I left, I told him I wanted to help him in any way I could. I didn't know what that meant, but I felt the need to say it. That would begin years of long-distance friendship. Through his undergraduate and graduate schools, we kept in touch. I loved tracking his story and how it evolved. Eventually, he found an incredible woman and seemed happier than he'd ever been. A year after they married, a beautiful son was born. His dreams had come true. But it was days after their son's first birthday that he found his wife passed away at home from complications of high blood pressure.

When I got the news, it broke me in half. Difficult things happen all the time, but there are instants that strike us close that can make us question the framework of the world. My brother's pain did that. As we wrote back and forth, I told him I loved him and prayed for him, and I'd send over some help. But was there anything he needed? Off the cuff, I asked if he wanted me to come to Nigeria. I wasn't against it, but I don't think I expected him to say yes. When he replied with, "Please do, we can talk more when you're here," I knew I had no choice. A month later, I was in Plateau State. He sat with me on the couch, introduced me to my godson, and told me how hard it was to wake up in the night having forgotten she was gone.

I didn't know why I was there, but I knew I needed to be. Days of walking and talking became laughing and dreaming, and by the time I left, our lives were not the same. He worked out a business plan for a farm. It had been the dream of his late wife for them to have their own business. We became partners. A chance interaction with a professional football coach I had met six years earlier led to a conversation and planning for the first independent professional football (soccer) academy in Jos. It would give disadvantaged kids a professional shot while developing their hearts and minds as well. In the end, I decided we needed a Nigerian registered nonprofit to manage the academy and to start creating services and programs to help confront poverty, disease, and conflict. I also decided that my brother would run it all.

As my plane took off from Abuja, I marveled at all that had happened. I'd come to bring love and support to my brother, and I was leaving with a football team, a nonprofit, and a yam farm as well. What if we'd never met that day? Would I have come back? Would Nigeria matter to me like it does today? I'll never know. Life isn't found in the hypotheticals. There is no alternate route; there is only the path you pick. And it's the subtle turns that can have the most lasting impact. Be it the briefest kindness to Samir or a life of investment to Isaiah. Moments of kindness and generosity are the milestones that will keep you going to places no one has ever gone before. But the only way to find them is to follow the relationship.

Part 5

# THE DIRECTION OF YOU

# 19

# FOLLOW THE RELATIONSHIP

I would rather walk with a friend in the dark,
than alone in the light.

—*Helen Keller*

In my head, it was after 3:00 p.m. I'm not sure if it really was since I was just a little kid, but it was in the afternoon. There was a knock at the door, and Robert came in. My mother was surprised, but that could have been added to the rest of her emotions for the month. She'd been more upset than usual. There had been crying and heated words with my father for a few weeks. A Sicilian home isn't often described as calm, but this was extreme.

Children are better at picking up on emotions than the narrative driving them. The Sunday before Robert came to the door, I remember presenting my mom with my coloring page from Sunday school. A simple picture with a verse under it, she looked at it and began crying. She was always grateful for something for the fridge, but this wasn't her typical response. I didn't understand. And as Robert came to the door the following Friday and the adults began talking, there was more crying, and I still didn't understand. But what I didn't know then has been seared into my mind now. Robert and Louise Guptill helped save my life. In two hours, we would have lost our home.

We were behind on the mortgage. Dad was working multiple side jobs. This was after the mill had burned down. Every penny mattered. One bad month became two, and before long, the bank had had enough. My parents had until Friday at 5:00 p.m. to make the payment or lose the house. Foreclosure in a town of 900 people, no other bank for forty miles to help secure another place, no full-time job, and no family nearby to take us in, the cascading consequences are hard to imagine.

This had been the source of the month's sadness. Mom and Dad scraped everywhere and found nothing. You know there's something wrong when your mother dreads movie day at school. Greg and I were in grade school, and on movie day once a month, each kid was supposed to bring fifty cents to contribute to the cost of the film. She would cry and make us pull apart the couch to see if any change had fallen out of Dad's pockets as he slept in front of the TV. She did whatever it took to survive.

I believe in prayer but also in action.

I learned years later that one of the fights my parents had was after a moment of mom's desperation. Out of options, she went to the pastor of our local church. We were more than regulars there. When the doors were open and the offering plate passed, the Dauphinees could be found somewhere. Mom and Dad subscribed to the Bible's call to give the church 10 percent of your income and did so with conviction about the good it did for others. But on this Sunday after church, my mother went to the pastor and told him what was about to happen. She was distressed, and there was no way out. Could the church help us? She told me he said he sympathized, but that the church wouldn't help. She should go pray and ask God what she should do—as if she hadn't been praying for months. I believe in prayer but also in action. You can find both in the "good book." And thankfully, Robert knew the book well.

Our hopes had been raised and dashed in that last week as my uncle Joe called from Arizona to say he could send money, but in 1980 in Patten, Maine, there was nowhere to send money to. And by mail, it would never be delivered in time. We had reached the end. We would lose our house for want of fifty dollars. And as the Friday deadline approached, every option had closed, until Robert opened the door.

My mother cried as he handed her the cash. How was this possible? How could he do this? The Guptills had little more than we did. There was no way they had extra money to give a friend. There wasn't any extra; he'd sold two cows from his herd to make our mortgage payment. It wasn't just a choice: It was an act of courage, and it was one that changed my life.

After some time, my mother took my Sunday school picture and put it in a simple frame over the door in our house. It was years before I realized the connection. But I can still see it in my mind's eye, and now I understand my mom's tears. At the start of the darkest week of her life, her young child had presented her a picture that said, "Your heavenly Father knows what you have need of." And while we needed prayers, we needed courageous action as well. We needed people like Robert and Louise who understood that, at the end, when all else fails, to move in the direction of you is to follow the relationship.

## When All Else Fails

I want you to be free. I want you to know you don't have to follow someone else's path. I want you to know it's not too late. You are not too broken. You're not a victim. You're not a prisoner; your cell door locks from the inside. And while there is an ever-clarifying destination that is you, and you'll seek to understand it the rest of your life, the direction is all you need to worry about. With every step, you get closer or farther from you. It's that simple. But yet it's not. And for those moments when you're exhausted, when you've demagnetized your compass, and you think you can't make another decision, I offer you my motto for life: Follow the relationship.

Follow the relationship when creating your calendar. Follow the relationship when deciding how to spend your money. Follow the relationship when you don't know what to do. If you've done the work of intentionally cultivating the people around you, moving toward them, investing in them, and seeking to be an increasing part of their life, you will be drawn forward. It won't provide all the answers, but it can nullify many questions.

I've been working for myself for thirteen years, years that include the Great Recession. I've done this without a business degree, without having studied entrepreneurship, and without having a large support team. In the early days, I wrestled with how to market and build a growing book of business. Every time the sales funnel emptied, I'd start to stress and spin up some tactic that came from someone's fail-proof list. I've hired people I was sure were smarter than me. I've paid for websites that were going to sell me. I've spent hundreds of thousands of dollars, sure that the gold of business success was found in some other person's genius. Then one day, a friend asked me to name my most successful clients.

Like an obsessed genealogist, I mapped out my business family tree. The trunk of the tree led back to that sad morning on the off-ramp to HP all those years ago. But it began growing from there. A conversation a few months later with the only Clifton

Strengths teacher I knew, Brian Schubring, led me to relocate to Minneapolis. He didn't offer me a job, but it was a chance to be a part of something different, and I thought it would help expand my possibilities. Over time, we began working together and accomplished things neither could have done without the other. Brian introduced me to Vantage Point Three and CA International. And as I stepped out on my own ...

VP3 led to
Eagle Sports, which led to
United Way, which led to
Fiat-Chrysler Automobiles, which led to
The Detroit Lions, which led to
Shinola Detroit
and so on.
CA International, which led to
Morgan & Sandy Davis, who led to
Silk Road Solutions, which led to
American University of Afghanistan, which led to
Coffey International, which led to
the Afghan Ministry of the Interior
and so on.

There are forks off these main branches, but you get the point. I've learned that good strategy is essential and I like when I plan more. But the days of beating myself because my approach to business is more relationships than business school are over.

In the last couple years, this relational approach has taken on an increasing radicalization. It has led me to countries I never planned on visiting and a business I had no intention to invest in. And client engagements, done initially at a discount as a favor, have matured in value and return. In fact, the publishing of the book only came after choosing to prioritize an invitation from one of my oldest clients and friends to be a part of his graduating son's "Words of Wisdom BBQ." I canceled a meeting and changed my flight to be there for my friend's gift to his son. That night, after sharing some thoughts, I was invited by an uncle to speak to his company. Turned out to be a publisher. I shared my heart over lunch and developed some new friendships. And now I'm chasing down this publishing deadline.

*An extraordinary life cannot be lived alone.*

I've heard it said that relationships are a great way to start a business but a horrible way to grow one. Good thing life isn't a business. Following the relationship is a posture that you can begin to develop that will cost you little but offers a vast reward. There's great truth to the old saying, "To find a friend, show yourself friendly." And you need wise friends. You can see the thread of relationships running through each chapter of this book. That's because an extraordinary life cannot be lived alone. Although the world drives to isolate, insulate, and tell you that you're nothing without what they're selling, the truth is the opposite. I saw it firsthand last year.

## The Lesson of Virginia

I was back in Jos, Nigeria, after the death of my friend's wife. I spent about two weeks there. I was there to encourage him, but I was happy to help out others if I could. I was going to do some teaching at the local hospital during afternoons. The founding director always welcomed internationals, but I've since learned of his manipulations as well. After an unexpected free morning, I asked him what I should be doing. In what I now realize was a setup, he told a couple of the young guys to "take Mike along. He can assist and preside over the funeral." Happy to help, I agreed. I've spoken words at memorials before, but this was a first.

I jumped in the pickup, and we drove off to the morgue to collect the woman who had passed away. I learned from the driver that she had been a refugee from the violent extremism in the northern state of Borno. She had come to Jos with nothing but a single friend. They settled in a squatter's neighborhood. She wasn't there long when she began to get sick. Her friend abandoned her there, never to be heard from again. When she neared death, the neighbors, fearing disease, delivered her to the hospital where she died. Tuberculosis is still one of the biggest killers worldwide.

The hospital had paid for her embalming, and she was to be buried in their pauper's field, the cemetery for the indigent. But as we arrived at the morgue, I learned she had died more than a month ago. The police wouldn't release the body until the neighbors came to identify her. It took four weeks and a police threat to get the three women and two men to come to the morgue that morning, so we could collect her body.

The paperwork wasn't right. There was back and forth between the witnesses and then a decision about who would dress her. The clothes they brought were rags. The men managed to find some rubber gloves before they carefully carried her month-old body out of the building on a steel morgue sled. Too long for the small pickup, she would have to ride to her final rest with the tailgate down and the neighbor boys as pallbearers.

But before we left for the field, one of the guys from the hospital realized the donated clothes were not enough to cover her. It was indecent. One of the women from the hospital went and begged for the dirty, stained sheet that one of the medical school students used as a curtain in their room on the campus nearby. With a borrowed shroud, one that wasn't long enough to cover her feet, we set off to pay our last respects.

I wish I could tell you that the truck didn't need to stop for gas. Or that her body wasn't lying there in the truck bed with the reluctant neighbors as they pumped the fuel. But it wouldn't be true.

Over the bumpy, potholed, red dirt road, we made our way to the field. Teen boys from the neighborhood nearby were paid to dig that day in the hot sun. And for a little extra, they'd serve as grave attendants as her plank-like body slid from the sled into the dry, dusty hole.

The woman from the hospital offered some words, but I don't remember what. My only memory is standing there looking down at this woman whose life had ended, and thinking to myself, where are her people? It was the only question that mattered. Someone gave birth to her. Someone loved her. Someone kissed her face. Where were her people? I didn't wonder about her job. I didn't care about her education. I had no concern for her race or tribe. I thought nothing about almost everything I offer people about myself. Where were her people? How could she be memorialized by a stranger she never met? How could she be leaving this life alone? At that moment, I knew there was no greater tragedy.

I hope you understand your identity. I hope you feel permission to dream of an extraordinary life and believe it. I hope you take courageous and sacrificial action. And I hope generosity fills you to never give up. But in the end, the questions you're going to ask are these: Where are my people? Who have I loved? Whose story have I changed? What questions will go unanswered because I'm not here to answer them? The only way to answer these extraordinary questions is by following the relationships.

After a prayer, before we started dropping handfuls of dirt, I realized that no one had said her name. I asked if anyone knew. With a sheepish look, one of her neighbors whispered, "Virginia." As I dropped a handful of dirt, I said "Thank you, Virginia. Your life mattered, and your passing has changed me."

# Where Does This Leave Us?

Sitting here at the end, I'm pondering my final words. It all comes back to my dad. He's not a saint and has never been a perfect father. He is as human as the rest. But for all his shortcomings, he gave me something that has transformed my life: an unshakable sense of self. It was a mix of hard work, faith, and pain, but I've never forgotten his admonition when he was disappointed in our behavior: "You can never forget you're a Dauphinee." It wasn't like we were Kennedys. Our name wasn't revered or well known, but there was a power to his point. Your life speaks for you and your family. Do you believe in what it's saying? It would take me years to separate out the value from the shame, but I now own it with pride.

I don't have to follow the expectations of others. I can make an investment of my time and money in my own way. I can declare my business successful, even though others will never want to buy it. I love that the name Dauphinee is now more known. It's becoming connected with strengths and identity. It's something I love moving closer to every day.

But what about you? Does your name mean something? Do your days tell the story of you?

If you can take hold of your compass, keep it calibrated, and in front of you, there's no obstacle or circumstance you can't navigate. You'll never be lost. And unlike Virginia, when your people come to say goodbye, like my dad on our ride years ago, they'll pause, smile, and say, "What an extraordinary life."

# About the Author

**Michael Dauphinee** helps leaders navigate their greatest challenges. After finishing college, a stint working in juvenile drug rehab and six years with Hewlett-Packard convinced him he had to work for himself. Founding the Dauphinee Group in 2005, Michael became one of the world's most sought-after strengths consultants, training and coaching at companies like Fiat-Chrysler Automobiles, the Bill & Melinda Gates Foundation, The Detroit Lions, the US Olympic Committee, Upside Travel, Kaiser Permanente, Chick-fil-A, and United Way Worldwide.

In 2010, Michael expanded into international development, specializing in security, governance, and justice in fragile and conflict-affected environments. He currently coaches entrepreneurs, embassies, universities, and governments in Nigeria, Honduras, Costa Rica, El Salvador, and Afghanistan.

Inspired by his trek through Torres del Paine in Chilean Patagonia, Michael founded Dauphinee Adventures in 2013. Clients have trekked hundreds of miles with him in Chile, Peru, and Nepal while wrestling with their most significant questions.

Always looking for ways to inspire others to navigate their lives courageously, Michael is a popular keynote speaker and shares daily inspiration online. Connect with him at michaeldauphinee.com.